Matthew M.
LOVEBIRDS

Everything about Housing, Care, Nutrition,
Breeding, and Diseases

With a Special Chapter: Understanding Lovebirds

Color Photographs by Outstanding Animal Photographers
and Drawings by Fritz W. Köhler

BARRON'S

New York / London / Toronto / Sydney

The photographs on the covers show

Front cover: A pair of Nyasa lovebirds *(Agapornis p. lilianae)* Inside front cover: Fischer's lovebird *(Agapornis p. fischeri)* Inside back cover: A pair of Fischer's lovebirds Back cover: Various mutations of the masked lovebird *(Agapornis p. personata)*

All inquiries should be addressed to:
Barron's Educational Series, Inc.
113 Crossways Park Drive
Woodbury, New York, 11797

International Standard Book No. 0-8120-3726-X
Library of Congress Catalog Card No. 86-10808

Library of Congress Cataloging-in-Publication Data
Vriends, Matthew M., 1937–
Lovebirds: everything about housing, care, nutrition, breeding, and diseases.
Bibliography; p.
Includes index.
1. Lovebirds. I. Title.
SF473.L6V74 1986   636.6'865   86-10808
ISBN 0-8120-3726-X
Printed in the United States of America

Photographers

Ardea/Fink: page 64, below. Brockmann/Wiching: page 27, above left and right, below left. Dossenbach: page 64, above. Lantermann: page 27, below right. Okapia/Dürk: page 63. Reinhard: front cover; inside front cover; back cover; page 9; page 10, above right, below right; page 28; page 45; back cover. Scholtz: page 10, above left, below left; page 46; inside back cover.

Matthew M. Vriends

The author of this book is a Dutch-born biologist/ornithologist who holds a collection of advanced degrees, including a Ph.D. in zoology. Dr. Vriends has written over eighty books in three languages on birds and other animals. Well known are his detailed works on lovebirds, parakeets, and finches. Dr. Vriends has traveled extensively in South America, the United States, Africa, Australia, and Europe to observe and study birds in their natural environment and is widely regarded as an expert in tropical ornithology and aviculture. A source of particular pride are the many first-breeding results he has achieved in his large aviaries, which house over fifty tropical bird species. Dr. Vriends and his family live on Long Island, New York.

Contents

Preface

Books can't teach a person how to become a pet lover. Love of pets is inborn. As children, pet lovers keep beetles in glass jars, bring home tadpoles and lost dogs, or try in vain to raise a baby bird that has fallen out of the nest. Once they become adults, they can't forget the animals they loved in their childhood, and soon there is a canary singing in their den, or there is an aquarium installed by the window, or an aviary appears in their yard.

A general love of animals can develop into a specific interest in lovebirds through some event or development. Some people are attracted to these birds because of their charm, behavior, and brilliant coloration. Others hear from friends about lovebirds' many other appealing traits.

Lovebird hobbyists usually start by acquiring a few birds, and then—on the advice of a friend—the hobby expands with an attempt to raise a nest of young. Frequently, hobbyists are encouraged because their first attempt is so successful. Not that such initial successes come about through dumb luck; beginning breeders have the enthusiasm to do the key things with the proper care.

When they see the dividends, most hobbyists will decide to continue. Almost without being aware, they fall under the spell of these decorative, enjoyable birds. They are drawn into the breeding game by seeing a color in, for example, peach-faced lovebirds, that is especially appealing. They get into trading and buying. They add cages or aviaries. Before they know it, they are up to their ears in lovebirds!

Keeping lovebirds means forgetting your worldly concerns by becoming absorbed in a pleasant avocation. Bird fanciers develop a sense of beauty and an appreciation for the pleasures to be found right at home. In most cases, they are scarcely aware of this. They keep lovebirds because they enjoy it, and don't give the matter further thought. One thing is certain: they wouldn't give up lovebirds for ''all the money in the world.''

This book could never have been written without the help of experienced breeders who followed the development of the book with interest. Their experience and knowledge, as well as their expert advice, are woven into the text.

I am particularly grateful to my friend, colleague-biologist, and countryman, Mr. Max B. Heppner, M.Sc., of Takoma Park, Maryland, for his invaluable assistance in the preparation of the text.

A special word of thanks to my wife, Lucia Vriends-Parent: her knowledge of the tropical and subtropical bird world never fails to astound me. She has consequently contributed much data that have been worked into the text. It was never too much effort for her to accompany me on the occasional lengthy and therefore tiring excursions into the interior of Africa. Without her it would have been impossible to write this and any other bird book.

A special thanks must go to my daughter Tanya M. Vriends, for her cooperation on this project, especially when it came to taking care of our birds! Thanks!

All the opinions and conclusions expressed in the following pages are my own, however, and any errors must be my own responsibility.

M.M.V.
Soyons fidèles à nos faiblesses
For Lucia and Tanya, with love

Considerations Before You Buy and Immediately After Purchase

In the wild lovebirds occur in groups, and partners often mate for life. They are well known for the care and affection they show toward their young, which they often continue to protect and feed after they have left the nest and are supposed to be independent.

Lovebirds combine efforts when searching for food and water, caring for the young, and fleeing from their enemies. But that is not all. They can be very cheerful, companionable, and tender toward one another. These traits are a major factor that have made lovebirds, and psittacines in general, such beloved and popular pets.

For over a hundred years lovebirds have proven to be excellent pets. They can easily be encouraged to breed in captivity, are suited for breeding new color mutants, and have even been known to speak a word or two, though this is rare.

To have a good pet, you must be a good master. You need to watch your birds closely without disturbing them. Look for unusual behavior and reactions, as this will tell you if anything is lacking in their care. I consider it

Lovebirds spend a lot of time grooming each other's feathers (preening).

a moral obligation to do all you can to keep pet birds as comfortable as possible.

Are You Sure Lovebirds Are for You?

You may already be a bird fancier, or you may become one. But before you buy any lovebirds, you must make the commitment to be or become good at the hobby.

I am serious about this. If you have birds and find you're not a fancier at heart, dispose of them. If you think you might get rich from breeding lovebirds, forget it. If you think that breeding lovebirds is a simple thing, think again.

The reverse is also true. If you are attracted to birds in general and lovebirds in particular, don't hold back. If you don't mind putting energy into the hobby, go to it. If you see yourself as a lovebird fancier and breeder, you *can* be one. Just don't lose your enthusiasm at the first sign of problems.

Be aware that the hobby costs money—but how much is largely up to you. If you're the type who gets into things big, you will need big money, particularly to start. It is expensive to have cages and aviaries built, especially if you choose top materials.

Starting the hobby with a modest investment is quite possible, however. A breeding cage is enough to keep one or two pairs of lovebirds, especially the more common species. And you can upgrade facilities and birds from the proceeds of your hobby if you breed young for trade or sale. I am convinced that a modest budget is enough to build up a fine stock, with adequate housing.

The amount of money needed for feed is not so great, either, provided you keep your

Considerations Before You Buy

initial stock of birds small. You do need to count on providing extra feed while your birds are feeding their young.

Can you actually make money from your hobby? A modest profit is at least a possibility. First, you will have to become good at it. You will have to spend considerable time and devote considerable space to the hobby.

Is a sizable profit possible? In theory, yes. But, as I said, don't count on it. Remember, it should be a hobby first, or else you will never stick with it. You are headed in the wrong direction if you see your birds principally as a source of income.

Having said all this, I won't deny that if you are a successful breeder and expand your hobby from your gains, you will acquire a lot of stock that represents a sizable investment. And if you sell young birds, you have every right to a reasonable profit.

If your luck holds, you can gradually start earning a nice amount from your lovebirds. You will be buying things as you go along without realizing it, and then you can be pleasantly surprised at the money coming in at the end of the year. Consider this money a windfall. Don't start counting on it. If you do, it will spoil your hobby.

There are all kinds of hobbyists. Some like it big. Their joy comes from having sheer numbers of birds around. Others like the unusual. They are the ones who strive for color mutations. They'd rather have a few really beautiful birds than a lot of common ones. These are the purists. They spend little time worrying about profits. I think they're the happiest with their hobby. For them, the hobby is what it should be: a pleasant way to spend their free time.

I have known people with a variety of approaches to the hobby. One woman has a breeding cage in her den and loves to watch the miracle of hatching and raising young birds from up close. One man is happy just to keep a single pair of birds in a cage on the windowsill. Another man has a small piece of land in the city; he decided to build a small aviary there and breeds lovebirds. Each of them is a true fancier. Each enjoys his or her birds, cares for them lovingly, and experiences them with possibly even more joy than the fancier who keeps a hundred birds.

Let me make a few special points about lovebirds to avoid misconceptions and difficulties if you want to start bringing these birds into your home or yard.

Lovebirds are among the most interesting birds. You will be fascinated by their behavior. Don't expect them to learn all kinds of tricks or imitate behavior. For that you should get a large parrot or a budgie.

- Lovebirds are social birds; consequently, they should always be kept in pairs. Singletons tend to slowly pine away (see page 8).
- Lovebirds require more care than just providing them with daily feed and water. First,

To be able to scratch its head, the bird has to raise its leg over its wing.

Considerations Before You Buy

A startled lovebird will raise itself high on the legs and hold the feathers tightly against its body.

you must provide these supplies at set times. Second, you must have set times to clean the cage or aviary. You will have to clear hulls from the floor around the "home." You will have to sanitize breeding and sleeping boxes, perches, and so on. Count on constantly having to do something for your birds.

● Lovebirds can be irritating if you don't like chatter. They chatter all day long, and this can grate on your nerves. Check this point by spending some time at a pet shop, bird show, or zoo exhibit. Do you hear song, or do you hear noise? Don't forget to include your family in this excursion, and don't forget to check with the neighbors before you start building an outside aviary. They may not be as crazy about birds as you are.

● The hobby costs money. Don't forget to budget for birds and for their upkeep, which will cost more than the initial investment. Your budget must include funds for a daily, richly assorted diet and for buying and replac-

ing sleeping and breeding boxes and perches. Be sure you can buy a large enough cage or aviary. Cramping your birds is cruel, and lovebirds need plenty of room (see page 18).

● Count on medical bills. Lovebirds are relatively sturdy, but there may be times you have to consult an avian veterinarian, and such services don't come cheap.

● Plan for a "pet sitter." Someone will have to care for your birds when you are sick or on vacation. Find out who is willing and able to do this for you among the people in your family, your circle of friends, or your neighbors. Consider all these points carefully. They are all important!

A final word of advice: start simple. Get a pair of common lovebirds to begin with, not a pair of expensive, rare mutants. Consider them a test. They can teach you how to care for them in and out of the breeding season; how to care for the young; and what they need in the way of housing and equipment.

Let's be realistic. You may begin with enthusiasm for all the care you need to provide, and then find that the enthusiasm pales. Not everyone develops into a first-class fancier. If you notice, even after a year or two, that breeding and keeping birds is not in your blood, you don't have to worry if you started simply. You won't have a lot invested in your hobby. If, on the other hand, you find that after a couple of breeding seasons your enthusiasm has increased, you can easily expand. You can "graduate" to the ranks of the true fancier.

Lovebirds in Your Home or Garden

I house every lovebird pair I own in an outdoor aviary that is exclusively theirs. Peo-

7

ple seem to expect an aviary to be stocked with a rich variety of birds. If you are planning to keep lovebirds, this is not recommended. I strongly suggest that you don't place lovebirds with other bird species, such as cockatiels, rosellas, or finches.

If you insist on trying to put more than one species in an aviary, you absolutely must have plenty of space. Each pair should have at least 35 cubic feet (1 m³) of space and adequate opportunity to flee if threatened. The aviary must be placed in a truly quiet location, so that dogs, cats, other pets, wild animals, and street traffic won't disturb the birds. Even with all these precautions, believe me, there is a distinct possibility that you will have quarrels, if not true fights (see page 37).

The most tolerant species of lovebirds are the black-cheeked lovebird and the Nyasa lovebird (see page 74). You can put them in colonies with other lovebirds and even with other bird species, provided they have plenty of room. If you have the space, you can try placing other lovebird species together, too. But whatever you do, never put two pairs together; it must be three or more couples in order to avoid fights.

You also need to make special arrangements. Each pair of lovebirds needs at least two sleeping and breeding boxes. All boxes must be of the same type and size. They must be hung on the same wall at the same height. There must be no extra males or females (hens); all pairs should be two birds of the opposite sex. If you aren't certain of the sex of all birds, take no chances. Place the doubtful cases in a separate cage and have the sex checked (see page 11).

Lovebirds must stay paired. If one partner is removed for any reason, you must get it a new partner as quickly as possible. Don't expect, however, that the new partner will be immediately accepted (see page 59). Be sure that you get a written statement from the person selling the replacement that you can exchange the bird if it doesn't meet your needs.

Outdoor breeding is apt to be the most successful; however, if the climate is too harsh, you may consider raising lovebirds indoors. Stick to a single couple if you're going to keep birds in a (breeding) cage. If you have a really roomy indoor aviary, heed the same precautions that I listed for an outdoor (garden) aviary. Never overstock! I think that three or at the most four couples are the absolute limit for an indoor aviary.

A Single Lovebird or a Pair?

Lovebirds are extremely social by nature. Many lovebird species probably pair for life, and the company of the mate is important in their lives. Just take a close look at the behavior of a pair of lovebirds. You will quickly see that they always sit next to each other. If one moves to a branch, the other follows. If one flies to the top of the sleeping box, the other immediately follows. In the breeding season, the male feeds his mate beak to beak after performing his mating dance. At times, the partners have shadow fights with their beaks. Nothing has gone wrong. They just do it for fun, to pass the time and to strengthen the bond between them.

If you keep a solitary bird, *you* have to make up for all this interaction it misses. You

Lovebirds of the white eye-ring group. Above, left: masked lovebird. Above, right: black-cheeked lovebird. Below, left: Fischer's lovebird. Below, right: Nyasa lovebird.

will never match what another lovebird could do. That's impossible, even if you spend many hours with it every day. If you live by yourself and stay home a lot, you could give it a try, but I think you'd be better off trying an experiment like this with a cockatiel, a budgie, or a cockatoo.

Lovebirds raised by hand are a special case. They are extremely attached to the "hand that fed them" and consider that person a partner, possibly because their own parents abandoned them for some reason. But that doesn't mean that hand-fed birds are friendly and tame toward other people. Nothing is further from the truth. If outsiders intrude on lovebirds, they are likely to get a painful bite on the hand, cheek, or ear.

In short, I won't tell you that keeping a single lovebird is cruel. I will say, however, that a pair is a far better choice than a singleton.

Sexing Lovebirds

With many species of lovebirds, sexing presents no problem. The sexes are clearly differentiated in outward appearance. Birds can be classified on this basis as belonging to the sexually dimorphic group (clearly different); the intermediate group (harder to differentiate by appearance); and the white eye-ring group (no consistent difference).

The Sexually Dimorphic Group

● Abyssinian lovebird (*Agapornis taranta*). Males have bright red feathers on the fore-

The four lovebirds on this page lack the prominent bare eye ring. Above, left: Madagascar lovebird. Above, right: Abyssinian or black-winged lovebird. Below, left: peach-faced lovebird. Below right: red-faced lovebird.

head and a few more bright red little feathers forming a very narrow ring around the eyes. Females (hens) have a small, greenish eye ring and a green forehead of the same shade as the rest of the body. The male has brownish black flight feathers and lesser wing coverts; the female's are gray-brown, sometimes with black markings. In young hens, these parts are greenish in color, but in young males these parts are black from the start. There is a slight weight difference between the sexes. Males average about 1.6 ounces (44 grams), and hens average about 1.9 ounces (53 grams).

● Madagascar lovebird (*Agapornis cana*). Males have a completely gray head and neck. The underwing coverts are black. The female is entirely green; there is no gray or black on her anywhere. There is no weight difference between males and hens.

● Red-faced lovebird (*Agapornis pullaria*). Males have an orange-red forehead and facial area, a light blue rump, and black flight feathers and lower wing coverts. The hen has green lower wing coverts with yellower edges to the wings. The forehead and facial area are more orange than red.

The Intermediate Group

● Black-collared lovebird (*Agapornis swinderniana*). Males and hens are similar in appearance.

● Peach-faced lovebird (*Agapornis roseicollis*). Males and hens are similar in appearance, although many females have a paler head.

The White Eye-ring Group

● Nyasa lovebird (*Agapornis personata lilianae*). Males and hens are similar in appearance, although hens often have more substantial beaks and are darker in coloration. There also is a slight difference in weight; males average about 1.3 ounces (38 grams), and hens average 1.5 ounces (43 grams).

● Black-cheeked lovebird (*Agapornis personata nigrigenis*). Males and hens are similar in appearance. There is a slight difference in weight; males average about 1.3 ounces (38 grams), and hens average 1.5 ounces (43 grams).

● Fischer's lovebird (*Agapornis personata fischeri*). Males and hens are similar in appearance. There is a slight difference in weight; males average about 1.7 ounces (49 grams), and hens average 1.9 ounces (53 grams).

● Masked lovebird (*Agapornis personata personata*). Males and hens are similar in appearance. There is a slight difference in weight; males average about 1.8 ounces (50 grams), and hens average 2 ounces (56 grams).

Note: Only females (hens) of the white eyering group carry pieces of nesting material tucked under the feathers of the rump and the lower back.

With birds that have no clear external sex differences, sexing is more difficult. People have used a number of methods, such as those listed below.

● *Body build*. Hens tend to be sturdier and heavier in build than males. This is not an absolute, however. With variations in nutrition, selective breeding, and other environmental factors, birds of the same sex may differ considerably in build.

● *Coloring*. Males often are thought to have somewhat more intense coloring than females. Again, this is no sure thing. Feed, breeding, climate, and geographical variations can significantly affect coloring.

● *Nest building*. Construction activities of the female are more intensive than those of the male. The hens gnaw out nest holes in thick branches and trunks, and they collect strips of bark for nest building. Perhaps as a result, they have a stronger grip than males, and if you handle them, they'll bite harder. Males tend to leave most building activities to the female, and they support the process mostly by feeding their female partner. Again, don't take this as an absolute. I have known several males that took an extremely active role in nest building, both in captivity and in the wild. Some people say that females tend to sleep inside the nest block and the male on top of it, but I think that's far from true.

● *Perching*. Hens sit more broadly on their perch. Their legs are spread apart more than

In many lovebird species, it isn't easy to distinguish males from females. Generally, the females sit more broadly on the perch, with the legs spread further apart. You can observe this well when a couple sit side by side on a horizontal perch.

those of the males if they are relaxed and healthy.

• *Tail flaring.* The tails of the sexes flare differently when they meet for mating and other social activities. The flare is slight, but distinct by sex. A hen gives you the impression that all the tail feathers are the same length; a male holds the tail feathers slightly nipped. The male, therefore, seems to have a rounded tail, and the female appears to have a tail that is trimmed straight across (see illustration, below). I consider this a fairly reliable indicator.

Typical tail postures can help determine the sex of a bird.

• *Anal inspection.* Birds have two thin, long, small bones, called *ossa pubes*, on the ventral side of the pelvis. These bones slant downward and to the rear. In grown females that have come into breeding condition, these two bones become more elastic and spread outward more, due to the effect of estrogen hormones. The bones are clearly further apart, and you can feel this with your fingers. In males, by contrast, the space between the two bones remains quite narrow; it seems as if the two bones lie right up against each other. This technique works only while females are sexually active. Hens that are not in breeding condition have their bones tightly joined, just like males.

• *Endoscopic examination.* Veterinarians can examine your birds with an instrument, the endoscope, which is inserted through the anus (cloaca) to directly inspect the internal organs. This technique works best for larger birds, although it works satisfactorily with masked lovebirds. Others are too sensitive to shock and stress to tolerate the endoscope.

• *Scientific examination.* Small samples of tissue or hormones can be examined in the laboratory to give a precise sex determination.

Lovebirds and Children

Most children love pets. Large parrots get their attention easily. Children are amused by their movements, they love the bright colors in the feathers, and they are fascinated if the birds can talk.

Lovebirds are not as suited as pets for young children compared with budgies or large parrots. I've mentioned several times that lovebirds form strong pairs and should be kept as such (see page 8), although this causes them to become more absorbed in each other and less interested in their environment or in their keepers, including children.

Older children, however, can enjoy lovebirds—let's say children aged 10 years and older. They will spend hours watching the interesting behavior of lovebirds in a cage or aviary. They will get even more out of it if they are guided and encouraged by experienced adults. Children must be told that lovebirds ordinarily can't be carried around the room on a shoulder or finger. They don't learn a repertory of tricks, and they don't imitate sounds. The children should learn to become interested in the lovebirds' fascinating behavior.

Who Will Look After Your Lovebirds When You Go on Vacation?

You may have heard people sigh, "I would love to have a pet, but if I get one I'll lose my freedom. Who will look after it when I go on vacation?"

They have a point. In many ways, pets tie you down. The alternate caretaker must be familiar with the requirements of your pet. You can't automatically depend on someone else in the family, a neighbor, or a friend to take over for you.

In short, you must make advance provisions. You could consider moving your birds to an avian veterinarian, if this service is provided for a fee. This is out of the question if you keep a large collection of birds in an outdoor aviary. Furthermore, lovebirds don't like being moved or taken somewhere by car. They get out of sorts, suffer from stress, and often refuse to eat.

The best solution I know is to join a local bird club. You will be surprised how many other bird fanciers live in your immediate neighborhood. Talk over your needs, and I am sure they will help you provide for them. Naturally, this is a mutual relationship, and you will help out other club members when they need help.

Don't take for granted that an experienced bird fancier will automatically know what to do. Leave precise instructions. Also leave plenty of all the necessary feed. You can't expect that your helper will take the time and trouble to buy all kinds of feed that you could easily have bought before you left on vacation!

Home-bred Versus Imported Lovebirds

Birds imported to the United States must be quarantined for 30 days by the Animal and Plant Health Inspection Service (APHIS) of the U.S. Department of Agriculture. This agency describes the requirements as follows: "Pet birds will be kept in individually controlled isolated cages to prevent any infection from spreading. Psittacine birds, hence, lovebirds, will be identified with a leg band. They will be fed a medicated feed as required by the U.S. Public Health Service to prevent psittacosis (see page 57). Food and water will be readily available to the birds. Young, immature birds needing daily hand feeding cannot be accepted because removing them from the isolation cage for feeding would interrupt the 30-day quarantine. During the quarantine, APHIS veterinarians will test the birds to make certain they are free of any communicable disease of poultry. Infected birds will be refused entry; at the owner's option, they will either be returned to the country of origin (at the owner's expense) or humanely destroyed."

Another important note issued by USDA/APHIS deals with smuggling. It states: "If you're tempted to buy a bird you suspect may have been smuggled into the United States . . . don't! Smuggled birds are a persistent threat to the health of birds and poultry flocks in this country. Indications are that many recent outbreaks of exotic Newcastle

Considerations Before You Buy

disease were caused by birds entering the United States illegally. If you have information about the possibility of smuggled birds, report it to any U.S. Customs office or call APHIS at Hyattsville, MD (301)436-8061.''

The most commonly imported lovebird species are the peach-faced, the masked, and the Fischer's lovebird. They may come directly from Africa or via Europe or Japan. These birds are expensive and not always immediately ready for breeding. Don't get them if you are just starting the hobby. I recommend you buy only birds that have been bred in this country. They are accustomed to being around people, to living in captivity, and to eating the available feed.

Some states have special regulations or restrictions on keeping birds, so it pays to become informed on what is and isn't legal. Some require that birds be banded; others don't. You can get the required information by writing Import-Export Staff, Veterinary Services, APHIS, U.S. Department of Agriculture, Hyattsville, MD 20782.

Where to Buy Lovebirds

You shouldn't buy birds just any old place. You need to know with whom you're dealing. Don't blindly respond to an advertisement because there is no way to be sure what you'll ultimately come home with. Go to a pet store that has a good reputation and a fine selection of lovebirds, or see what the reputable breeders in your neighborhood have to offer.

Buy first-quality stock, even if you're a beginner. As I stated earlier, high quality doesn't mean superexpensive. Buy the best available individuals in the common lines of lovebirds.

Visit some local bird shows. Look in bird magazines for announcements of such shows in the fall of each year. This is the best way to see what is being done in the world of lovebirds. If you ask around, you will get the names of several dependable breeders and dealers. Also, take out a membership in the local bird club; people there also can advise you what and where to buy.

Get all the advice you can. It takes a trained eye to really see a lovebird. An experienced person can look at a bird and tell you a lot about its health and fitness, can hold and give you a dependable assessment about any defects, and even give you a pretty good guess as to its sex.

Here are a few factors to alert you to problems when buying lovebirds.
● Birds kept in dirty cages or aviaries: if the cages are poorly maintained, you can assume the birds are poorly maintained also.
● Birds offered at an extremely low price: they're probably smuggled and may be sick.
● Birds offered with little or no information about them that can be verified.
● Birds housed with many companions in a small enclosure.
● Birds with any defect or health problem.
● Birds that don't observe you alertly when you look them over.

How to Recognize Healthy Lovebirds

A healthy lovebird sits upright and alert on its perch. It has a clear, intelligent look in its eyes and a clean, tight cover of feathers. It doesn't allow other birds in its cage to peck it.

Feel free to take a prospective new pet in

your hand to examine it, but be careful. Lovebirds can inflict painful bites, so wear soft-leather gloves.

Look the bird over carefully, from beak to tail. Look at the beak; it must close completely and must be smooth on the outside. Look at the top of the head; there must not be any bald spot shimmering through the feathers. Look at the wings; there must not be any broken shafts. Look at each leg separately; they must look healthy and smooth, and the toes must be straight with all nails complete. Toes and nails are especially important in *males*; if they are missing a nail they can't mate effectively because they can't get a good grip on the back of their mate. Look at the tail; it must be clean.

Check the breast bone, which rises like a knife along the middle of the breast from top to bottom. Take off one glove for the examination, and palpate the bone carefully. Right and left of the bone, you should be able to feel firm flesh.

Examine the area around the cloaca. If you notice anything dirty and sticky, put the bird back. It probably has an intestinal problem.

Study the breathing. If you hear a squeak in the breath, suspect problems.

Blow into the feathers of the stomach and chest. The skin that is revealed must look healthy, not splotched or fiery red.

I'm not saying that if the bird shows any symptoms of deformity or illness that the bird is doomed to a speedy death. Many illnesses can be cured, and you should feel free to inform the seller of your findings and suggest an avian veterinarian be consulted. I am saying that as a prospective buyer you shouldn't buy trouble, or even accept it as a present.

Birds that have symptoms of disease are likely to be poor breeders or not fit for breeding at all. And even if you're not planning to breed, who wants to start with a sick bird?

I repeat: first and last, the best rule to follow if you're buying is never buy inferior stock. Buy only birds in top condition and first-rate health. Only those birds can meet your expectations.

The Trip Home

When you pick up a new lovebird, you acquire a creature that has just gone through a variety of stress. It has been looked over by various customers at the store or at the breeder. It has been short on rations and water and exposed to strange and scary noises. It has been netted, taken in hand, and finally placed in a box or traveling cage.

Then, like it or not, you add to the stress. You can't help but shake up the little creature on the way home, which tends to raise its body temperature. So make that trip home as short and expeditious as possible. If you go by car, guard against both heat and draft. Keep the traveling cage out of direct sunlight, and open the car windows enough for plenty of fresh air.

If you make the trip in cold weather (which I discourage), wrap the traveling cage in heavy wrapping paper. Be sure to make some ventilation holes in the paper. See to it that there is plenty of seed and soaked bread on the bottom of the cage.

On long trips, take at least a 20-minute break every three hours. Let the bird eat in peace from the seed and soaked bread. This will give it a chance to recuperate a little.

Considerations Before You Buy

The First Few Weeks

Here is some special advice to follow during the first few weeks as a new bird owner.

• Have your birds examined immediately after arrival by an avian expert (experienced fancier or veterinarian).

• Keep new lovebirds isolated from other birds for at least two weeks, preferably in separate rooms, in order to avoid spreading contagious diseases.

• Offer your new lovebirds a chance to relax. Avoid loud noises and harassment from other animals (such as barking dogs). Leave the birds alone as much as possible. Don't show the birds off to each and everyone. Early taming and training is a "no-no." Wait until the birds are completely acclimatized to their cage or room aviary and comfortable among people; avoid excessive handling at all times.

• House the lovebirds in a cage, *not* a round one, as it makes the birds nervous. The cage should be as large as possible—a minimum of 3 feet 3½ inches × 3 feet 2 inches × 2 feet (120 × 95 × 60 cm)—with some perches arranged so that ruffling of tail feathers can be avoided. Place the cage at eye level in a corner; this gives the birds a sense of safety and security.

• Maintain a stable temperature of approximately 80°F (27°C) during the first 25–30 days of new ownership. Use a heat lamp, or better still an infrared lamp. Avoid all sorts of portable heaters (fire risk). After approximately 30 days, lower the heat to room temperature very gradually over a period of 15–20 days.

• Avoid drafts, but maintain proper ventilation. Ideally, use a box cage, an opaque box constructed of thin metal or wood, with only an open front. It eliminates the danger of drafts and also gives the birds a sense of security.

• Besides providing the food the birds are accustomed to, furnish for 4 days (and only for 4 days!) a high-protein stress formula diet that is palatable. Diets that contain *Lactobacillus* predigested proteins (an easily metabolized source of quick energy), such as 8 IN 1 AVILAC, are preferable. Never change diets abruptly; do it gradually over a period of 2–3 weeks. Abrupt dietary changes often upset the digestive tract and are extremely dangerous.

• Don't provide sand and/or grit for at least 10–15 days, as stress conditions and anxiety trigger overeating. This could cause dangerous health problems. Maintain, however, proper hygiene!

• Lovebirds with an extremely nervous behavior—often with almost constant wing flapping—must be wing clipped (see page 44) in order to prevent serious bodily injuries and mental stress.

• Avoid total darkness at night; provide a small 7-watt night light, so the bird is able to find its perch and drink or feed cup at all times. Give the bird at least 10–12 hours of total rest. Don't forget fresh food and drinking water for the night.

• Avoid insecticides, paint fumes, smoke, open windows, long and direct sunlight (sunstroke), moldy grains, unwashed vegetables and fruits, and spoiled drinking water (use spring water at room temperature).

Housing and Equipment

Birds in your care should be well housed and well equipped. Give them plenty of room. In the wild, lovebirds are lively fliers that cover long distances on the wing every day and actively climb among the branches of trees and shrubs. In captivity, lovebirds that are squeezed for space rarely breed. They get fat and sluggish, become bored and pick feathers, and die before their time.

Lovebirds are keen climbers, so a climbing tree in the aviary has great therapeutic value. You can put together a climbing tree yourself. Take a big tub, fill it with soil and gravel (or rubble), and insert a thick fruit-tree branch; choose one with several side branches.

Young birds especially need freedom of movement. Therefore, I recommend housing newly independent birds in roomy runs (flights) where they can fly about to their heart's content. This allows them to develop their muscles, lungs, and other organs more fully. After the breeding season, it is also desirable to let the breeding pairs get some recreation to make up for the stressful period they've just experienced. Give them some time in the runs also, if at all possible.

Cages

Sturdy cages with a trellis all around are available commercially in many sizes. For a single pair, the minimum cage size is 3 feet 11 inches × 3 feet 2 inches × 2 feet (120 × 95 × 60 cm). Generally, these cages come with four perches. Place these inside the cage in a way that prevents the birds from scraping against the trellis when they turn about; you don't want them to damage their tail feathers.

Never buy cages less than 2 feet 5 inches (75 cm) in length. This is no way to save money. Besides the many problems I've already mentioned, tight quarters can cause birds to screech, to fight, and even to kill one another.

For Madagascar lovebirds and black-cheeked lovebirds, you might consider a sturdy parakeet cage measuring at least 3 feet 3½ inches × 2 feet 7½ inches × 2 feet (100 × 80 × 60 cm).

The trellis should be no more than ½ inch (15 mm) apart. Birds can squeeze through openings that are wider. The trellis should always run horizontally, so that the birds can climb up easily.

Cages made of wood or synthetic material are no good for lovebirds. They will ruin the surface with their beaks in a short time.

Make sure the cage door closes tightly, preferably with a sturdy lock. Lovebirds often figure out how to open a latch and escape.

Always place cages in a bright, draft-free location. You might do well also to provide supplementary, indirect lighting.

Lovebirds are true parrots and love to climb. Some branches for them to climb on are therefore essential, but don't overdo this because birds also need to fly as much as they need to climb.

Attach nestboxes to one of the sides, projecting outward. This keeps the inside of the cage roomy and facilitates inspecting your birds.

This is a fairly decent cage but much too small for lovebirds (2 feet 3½ inches × 1 foot 7½ inches × 2 feet 3½ inches; 70 × 50 × 70 cm). Cages of this size or smaller should only be used if you can let out the birds daily to fly around the room.

Lovebirds like to gnaw wood. It's essential that you provide fresh branches daily, from fruit trees, willow, hazel, and other trees.

Get water and seed dishes made of earthenware or porcelain, so that the birds won't ruin them. They can destroy plastic in no time. For other equipment, refer to suggestions for vitrines (see page 20).

Breeding Cages

Cages meant for use only during the breeding season are available commercially in various models. They are open fronted, meaning that the front is made of mesh or trellis; the other walls and the roof and floor are made of metal, wood, or plastic and therefore are solid.

Lovebirds feel safer in breeding cages than in the more open trellis cages. They are also more protected from cold and drafts. Place the breeding cage in a well-lit location where unfiltered sunlight can shine in.

The minimum size is 3 feet 3½ inches to 3 feet 11 inches long; 3 feet 2 inches to 3 feet 3½ inches wide, and 2 feet to 2 feet 3½ inches high (100–120 cm long, 95–100 cm wide, and 60–70 cm high).

Some commercial models can be stacked next to or on top of each other, which isn't a bad arrangement for a bird room. With an arrangement of breeding cages, you don't need other housing. You can even use them to house the sexes separately after the breeding season, something I recommend with emphasis.

Some commercial models can be partially taken apart, so that you can make one large cage from, let's say, four small ones. Other types may have removable sides, making it easy to join the cages together by removing the common walls. Look over the possibilities at a bird show.

Perhaps you wish to construct a breeding cage. You can obtain fronts commercially. Buy one of the large sizes. If it isn't large enough for the roomy cage I recommend, construct a frame to make it fit. Build a removable tray into the bottom. If you're constructing several adjoining breeding cages, be sure the fronts have enough doors and openings to fill the drinking and eating dishes. You can construct breeding boxes against the sides or front of the cage. This simplifies health and safety checks without disturbing your birds.

Housing and Equipment

Vitrines

Vitrines simply are a finer type of box cage, made with a glass instead of mesh front. You can buy these commercially, assembled or in ready-to-assemble parts.

A pair of lovebirds should be given a vitrine of at least 3 feet 11 inches × 3 feet 3½ inches × 2 feet 1½ inches (120 × 100 × 65 cm).

You can build a vitrine from scratch, using plywood, treated hardboard, or PVC (polyvinyl chloride) interlocking plastic panels. Varnish or spray the interior, or paint it with lead-free paint. Consider a design so that the rear wall, side wall, and glass front can all be detached or slide apart. This makes the structure much easier to clean, a task that faces you at least once a week. Make a double groove in the frame in front of or behind the movable wall. Fit a piece of cardboard to run in the groove, so that you can remove the permanent wall for cleaning. Birds get used to this routine quickly.

The roof of the vitrine should be solid for two-thirds of its surface. The other third should be a tightly fitted window of mesh for improved ventilation. Mount artificial lighting into the roof, preferably a 10-watt fluorescent bulb. Place the light carefully; you don't want to have to stare at it from your usual position of observing the birds. Indirect lighting is best.

The floor should be a removable tray about 1–1½ inches (2½–4 cm) deep. Put a layer of grit, oyster shell, and sand in the tray. For perches, use several well-shaped natural branches of willow, poplar, hazel, or the like. Be prepared to replace these frequently, since the birds will gnaw them to pieces in a short time. Also get some commercial perches with a minimum diameter of ½ inch (15 mm). They are essential, especially during mating. Mount them solidly in the corners, so that the center of the vitrine remains open for free flight. Never place a perch directly above another; you don't want birds perching on the lower level to be fouled by the birds above.

Make openings in the sides for easy access to utensils. The openings should be large enough so your hand can go through easily. Mount dishes outside the vitrine to provide more room inside. Construct several doors in the sides (and even in the rear) so that you can easily service the needs of your birds. At any rate, never place the dishes under perches, as these will be fouled by droppings.

Indoor Aviaries

An indoor aviary is one that is situated in a room. You can buy several types of commercial kits that should work well for you. They are suitable for several pairs of lovebirds of the same species or of the same color mutation. (Remember, never house two pairs of lovebirds together!)

You may want to construct an indoor aviary from scratch. It should consist of a good-sized flight, with a high enough ridge on the edges on which to mount frames of mesh. The ridge keeps hulls, sand, and other dirt out of the room. Stain the ridge, frame, and similar surface, varnish them, or use a safe paint that harmonizes with the interior.

Blending the aviary into the room is a good objective. Find a relatively inconspicuous location, perhaps in a corner near a sliding glass door leading to the garden. Such a location is good because direct sunlight can enter the aviary, something the birds need and enjoy. Place a variety of plants around the aviary so that you have an integrated piece of nature in your home to enjoy year-round.

Furnish the aviary much like a bird room (see below).

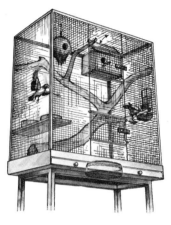

This indoor aviary, with closed back, measures 2 feet 7½ inches × 1 foot 7½ inches × 3 feet 3½ inches (80 × 50 × 100 cm), which provides birds the opportunity to stretch their wings.

Bird Rooms

A bird room is one that is totally dedicated to birds or, often, to the breeding of lovebirds. I think you'll like a bird room better than sectioning off part of a room with breeding cages, especially if you are working with a certain type of bird or color mutation. The more space birds have to fly around, the better it is for them.

Any room will do for a bird room, including a den or even a section of the attic, as long as it is sunny but not too hot or cold. It is important for the health of your birds that they regularly spend time in natural sunlight. They need ultraviolet light to build up body choles-

terol and convert it to provitamin D_3. The birds instinctively know what to do. As soon as they have a chance to sun themselves, they spread their wings and take a complete sunbath. Even if they can't sit in the sun, they tend to roost in the lightest places. That is why I recommend a good fluorescent light (Vita Lite) for indoor bird facilities.

With very little construction you can put together a dream of a bird room. Place screens in the windows so that unfiltered sunlight can enter. Put a few rustic-looking dead trees in pots, and anchor them down well with wet soil, giving the birds plenty of opportunity to climb around (see illustration, page 18).

It's essential that a bird room can be aired out thoroughly and regularly without creating a draft. Make it mouse and rat proof. Mice and rats can be kept out of the bird room and (indoor) aviary by placing small pieces of cloth soaked in peppermint oil in their holes and passages. It is a method passed down from my grandmother, and it seems to work! In any case, it is a harmless method, so there is nothing lost in trying. There are several poisonous products for mice and rats on the market and even products that are harmless to birds. Ask your exterminator for advice. I personally like my grandmother's method, regardless of the old-fashioned origin, as it is equally safe for people and birds.

Protect your birds against parasites by filling cracks in floors and walls with wood putty.

Cover the floor with construction-grade heavy plastic. Put a good layer ¾–1½ inches (2–4 cm) of sand over it; regularly rake the sand clean, and replenish it as necessary.

You can add a small fountain or pond. Use your imagination to bring an attractive piece of nature into your home. Indulge your taste to arrange and improvise.

Hang nestboxes (see page 29) along the wall at the same height and at least 23½ inches (60 cm) apart. Nestboxes should all be identical. If you see that your birds don't like a certain type, try another, but never have several types up at the same time. Lovebird pairs that see any difference between the box they want to use and those other pairs have available will start fights, without exception and without letup. You'll never get a good hatching. Fights and poor hatching also result from keeping just two pairs of lovebirds; this appears to be an unacceptable setup for them. Stick to the rule of one pair, or three pairs or more—never two.

Outdoor Aviaries

The outdoor or garden aviary should be built for permanence. Build it sturdy, to last a long time. You don't want the whole thing to blow over with the first breeze. Don't skimp.

Make your aviary as complete as possible before you stock it with birds. Later changes cause extra trouble. It is easier to make changes on paper than in reality, so think ahead with a complete building plan.

Birds are kept to be seen, so locate the aviary where you can watch the birds easily. Landscape the rest of the garden to integrate the aviary with the rest of the layout. You don't want the aviary to look lost, but rather, to be an integrated part of an attractive whole.

Orient the front of the aviary to the south as much as possible. If you have to deviate, southeast is better than southwest.

A good size for the run or flight of an outdoor aviary is at least 9 feet long (2½ m), 5 feet wide (1½ m), and 6 feet 6 inches high (2m). The night shelter should be at least 5 feet × 5 feet × 8 feet 2½ inches (1½ × 1½ × 2½ m). If you build several runs next to each other, be sure to leave a space of at least 2 inches (5 cm) between adjoining mesh walls. If you don't take this precaution, birds might bite each other's toes and legs.

Use metal in your construction, wherever birds can reach with their beaks. They will chew away on anything that's wood until they ruin it. Where you use mesh, select ½ inch × 1 inch (13 × 25 mm) mesh.

If you use glass anywhere (as for reducing drafts), use reinforced glass. Never use reflective glass. Birds like their reflections and have been known to fall in love with their own image. This plays havoc with your breeding.

Plan for good drainage. Poor drainage leads to wet floors, which in turn leads to trouble with internal parasites, molds, and other difficulties you are better off avoiding. So, the complete floor of the aviary should be at least an inch higher than the garden outside the aviary.

Construct both the covered and open sections on the foundation of a small wall, perhaps 23½ inches (60 cm) in total height, with 15½ inches (40 cm) underground and 8 inches (20 cm) aboveground. You can use brick or any type of cement block, which is cheaper. Put some rustproof framing into the foundation as you construct it, so that it's easier to anchor any future structures into the foundation. This way of building is truly solid.

Build the roof of the night shelter somewhat higher than the roof of the flight. Birds seem to like to spend the night at a higher level. Most lovebirds also prefer to sleep in their nestboxes, so hang these high in the covered part of the flight, or, better still, in the night shelter.

Don't close off the night shelter entirely. Birds don't like total darkness and will stay out of a dark shelter. So, build the roof with materials that will let light shine through, like corrugated PVC (the same material can be used to cover part of the run). Design the shelter with some large windows, but cover the window openings on the inside with mesh screens. That way, you can open the windows in good weather without the chance of birds flying out. The mesh also prevents birds from flying into the windowpanes, which they don't seem to notice; collisions with glass can cause serious injuries.

A well-lit night shelter keeps birds from chasing around at dusk, which tends to happen especially in aviaries holding several pairs of the same species. At dusk, birds become uneasy and begin searching for a good place to roost for the night. Generally, the various pairs have their favorite roosts, as a branch in a certain corner or in a sleeping or nestbox. If you follow my suggestion and place the boxes high in the night shelter, the birds will instictively fly into the shelter. If there is enough daylight left to find their favorite spot easily, they won't get into fights.

Your entire aviary should be rat and mouse proof (see page 21). Pave the floor with concrete, at least 2½ inches (6 cm) thick, or tile it. If you want to keep the natural soil, bury sheets of mesh about 16 inches (40 cm) under the surface. Old, used mesh is fine for this purpose; after you cover it with soil, no one will be able to see it. Be sure, however, to first rustproof the mesh.

Do what you can to discourage visits from cats, owls, raccoons, and other pets and wildlife. No precaution is excessive. A single invasion by a cat into the environs of breeding lovebirds can ruin a complete hatching.

Never install perches or anything birds might roost on near the wire mesh. If birds sit near the mesh, they are easier prey for cats and the like.

Don't have any tree branches overhanging the aviary from which animals could jump down. One good way to discourage animals from climbing up on the aviary is to stretch wire at several levels about 3½ inches (8 cm) away from the mesh. Build overhangs on all roofs. Consider installing electric fencing around the entire aviary. Electric fences aren't harmful, even to small animals like cats, but a jolt from touching one sends them a lifelong reminder to stay away. Electric fencing doesn't come cheap, but your lovebirds should be worth it.

While we are on the subject of electrical installations, think about an alarm system. Remember, many thieves are "bird lovers," or vice versa, and there is no reason you should be the victim who meets their larcenous needs.

Put small doors into the night shelter and the flight; keep them so low that you can enter or reach in only on your haunches. The reason for low doors is that birds tend to fly off in an upward direction, so that only rarely will a bird fly past your shoulder if the opening is low. If you want absolute protection from escapes, build a safety porch. It has a door at both ends of an enclosed passage, so that you can close one end of the passage before opening the other. If any bird flies by you, it is still trapped in the passage or safety porch, and you can coax it back into the aviary.

Housing and Equipment

To paint the aviary, start with the inside of the night shelter. The best paint is a nontoxic white paint, which makes the shelter brighter and allows you to spot invasions by lice and other vermin more easily. You can paint the outside of the shelter with colored outdoor varnish, which helps preserve the wood. Choose a color that blends into the environment. You can also use carbolineum (creosote), but I hate it. It is a good preservative, but the bad smell persists and could harm your birds. In fact, any paint odor may be harmful. Let any paint in the aviary dry at least 7–10 days before you put birds in the place.

Paint all the mesh with brown outdoor varnish (or black bituminous paint). It retards rust and makes the fencing less conspicuous. Paint it on both sides. Keep the paint cover thin with a brush that is nearly dry, or use a roller. Also paint the wooden or metal uprights that hold the fencing.

The Right Location

Provide your lovebirds with plenty of light and fresh air, whether you raise them indoors or outdoors. Arrange it so that they get morning sun in as much of their enclosure as possible. This is why I suggest building an outdoor aviary, for example, with as much southern exposure as possible. Balance the need for fresh air with the need to protect birds from drafts, which are a big hazard and must be avoided. This is why glass could have a place in constructing outdoor aviaries. Don't use reflective glass (see page 22).

Environmental Requirements

Lovebirds are tropical birds, originating from Africa and Madagascar. They are accustomed to warm, humid climates. However, lovebirds can acclimatize to considerable cold and low humidity. The lower temperature limit seems to be 12°F (-10°C). The lower humidity limit seems to be 65 percent; if it drops below that level, birds will have trouble when laying eggs. Remember, however, that this problem may be dietary, so be sure the level of vitamin B complex in the diet is adequate (see Egg Binding, page 51).

There are some differences among species. Peach-faced lovebirds are hardy birds and can be kept outdoors year-round in much of the United States. They do need protection from wind, drafts, and rain, so the night shelter should be enclosed on all sides. Take the precaution, also, of setting up heat lamps in the shelter.

Fischer's lovebirds, masked lovebirds, and Abyssinians also are relatively hardy. If you have winters that are on the cold side, make sure they have a draft-free place to sleep, perhaps a small nestbox. Other species need heating and lighting in the night shelter, along with an enclosed run. In the winter, don't let any Nyasas, black-cheeked, red-faced, or Madagascar lovebirds in the outside run unless the weather really warms up. Personally, I wouldn't house red-faced lovebirds in outdoor aviaries, except in truly semitropical areas (Florida and Southern California).

The general rule is to move lovebirds indoors if you expect the temperature to fall below 12°F (-10°C). Even the hardiest birds should come indoors to a frost-free room when temperatures fall well below freezing.

Housing Requirements

Lovebirds are active birds that don't belong in a small cage or aviary. This is why you are urged to observe the minimum sizes listed for

Housing and Equipment

various enclosures. It is far better to err on the large side than to skimp on room. This applies especially to aviaries that hold several couples. Limited space leads to constant squabbling and to a ruined breeding season.

Don't change the enclosure after you have set it up and placed birds in it. This makes them uneasy. Take all possible precautions against a cage tipping over, but place it at a high level so birds can look down. The cages should be at least 6 feet off the floor. If you stack breeding cages that open into one another, it's okay to have the lowest cages on the floor; just keep the top cages high enough. When birds are actually breeding, however, they don't care at what level their cages are set.

Keep cages away from the television set. The direct rays could be harmful to the birds. The high sounds don't seem to bother birds like they do mammals, but you don't want to expose them to too much noise. They need to have at least 10–12 hours of rest, so they can sleep. If you must have a television in the same room with your lovebirds, cover the cage with a cloth at the appropriate time.

Perches

In the outdoor or indoor aviary and in the bird room, a few dead trees should be provided (see page 21). Also, some good-sized fruit tree branches, willow, hazel, poplar, birch and the like that have live twigs with leaf and/or blossom are necessary. Supply these on a daily basis if possible. This gives the birds some extra food as well as something to play with. Lovebirds also enjoy taking naps on live branches.

The need for perches should be balanced with the need for adequate flight space. It is better that your birds fly than that they spend the whole time climbing around on branches and wire mesh. This is why lovebirds need plenty of space.

Don't hang any perches or live, dead, or commercial roosts above the feeding or bathing area to avoid fouling. Don't place perches too high because you want to avoid damage of head feathers. And don't put perches near wire mesh or trellis, to protect the tail feathers.

In the night shelter of the outdoor aviary, place an adequate number of perches and nestboxes high off the ground (see page 23). If you buy any perches, make sure they are thick enough to prevent birds from closing their toes completely around them. Ordinarily, the perches should be at least ½ inch (15 mm) in diameter. The toes should be protected by the stomach feathers while the birds are resting. If toes are unprotected, they are more likely to freeze (see page 57). Be alert for frozen toes when the temperature drops below 22–26°F (-3 to -5°C), especially if the perches are too thin.

Make certain that all perches are firmly anchored. Swinging perches may be fun for the viewer, but they are bad for the birds. I say this, first, with an eye to effective breeding. Swinging perches make copulation difficult, if not impossible.

Second, swinging perches are a threat to the tail feathers. Lovebirds instinctively try to stop the swinging action when they land on a perch. They do this by spreading their tails and pushing them downward every time the perch swings forward. For every backward swing, they do the opposite. This places special stress on the tail muscles, which can cause the feathers to fall out. It is as if the

Housing and Equipment

feathers are being worked loose, slowly but surely.

It's worth getting a good picture of this in your mind. Here you have a group of lovebirds on a swinging perch and, hop, there comes an additional bird to join them. The landing process moves the perch forward, and all tails of the perching birds try to brake this forward movement, so that the birds keep their balance. The tails move forward and then backward until they still the movement of the swing. No sooner has this happened then one of the perching birds takes off, and swoosh, all tails are back in motion.

If you want to observe this reflex action up close, just take a single lovebird in your hand and drop your hand toward the floor, Then, raise your hand toward the ceiling. In other words, you make the bird dive down and rise. As this happens, watch the tail, and you will notice that it automatically moves along. It rises when the bird dives and is lowered during the upward motion.

Lighting and Heating

You need to equip the night shelter of the garden aviary with electricity. You won't need a bright light there; I recommend a night-light of 7 watts. You'll be glad to have the night-light when birds are disturbed or frightened at night. Their first reaction is to fly about in a panic, and they can easily hurt themselves in the process by flying into the mesh, wood, perches, and the like. With a night-light, they can avoid crashes and easily find their sleeping places again once they calm down. I recommend a night-light for the same reason in an indoor aviary or bird room.

The night shelter in the indoor aviary should be equipped with a few Vita Lites as an emergency heat source. These heat lamps are available from any good bird dealer or pet store. You never know when a sudden cold spell will make it important to heat the night shelter.

Food and Water Dishes

Consider only dishes made of porcelain or earthenware. Cheap plastic or wooden bowls are out, because lovebirds are inveterate gnawers and will ruin these dishes in no time. Get bowls up off the floor. Lovebirds in captivity don't like to eat at floor level, and food at floor level also attracts mice and other rodents. In cages, hang dishes from the trellis; in aviaries or bird rooms, place bowls on a platform about 13½ inches (35 cm) high.

You could consider commercially made drinking fountains constructed of hard plastic or glass. If you want to get these, be sure that they are easy to clean. Never buy dishes with edges that curve inward at the top. Birds, especially young, inexperienced birds, can accidentally get their beaks hooked under the overhang. Waterers that don't have algae sediment in them can be cleaned easily by putting some bicycle ball bearings in them and shaking them hard with rinse water. Take out the ball bearings, rinse again, and there you are!

Bathing

Lovebirds enjoy bathing, with the exception of the Madagascar lovebird and the red-faced lovebird. Just watch them frolic in a

In the "nursery" of the peach-faced lovebird. Above, left and right: nest with eggs and one chick—recently hatched. Below, left: young, about 10 days old. Below right: young approximately 19 days old.

Housing and Equipment

The waterer (left) and the seed dishes (right) are the correct type for a lovebird cage. They must be constructed of sturdy material, or the birds will gnaw them to pieces in no time. The small fragments could be very harmful if swallowed.

summer shower. For periods without rain, it is essential that they have access to bathing facilities—more than one in spacious aviaries. Naturally, birds kept indoors have to be given full-time access to a bath.

A good bird bath is a flat, earthenware dish with a raised edge. Lovebirds aren't the type that will stand in the water. Rather, they tend to sit on the edge of the bath and dip their head or upper body into the water. They also beat happily with their wings. They will spread their body feathers somewhat, so that the water can get to their skin.

In the case of wild Madagascar lovebirds and red-faced lovebirds, there have been sightings of them taking a lengthy shower in a light rain, their feathers spread, their head

Wild-colored and color mutations of the masked lovebird. Top (from left to right): blue, wild-colored, and white-blue. Bottom: wild-colored, yellow, and blue.

low, and their wings raised. So if you keep these species, check to see if they would enjoy a shower of that kind. Use a plant fogger with lukewarm water.

Bathwater in dishes must be kept clean and fresh. If not, the birds won't use it. Be aware, however, that lovebirds will drink from any water source, even if it is dirty. So, in this connection, let me stress the importance of providing them with fresh drinking water several times a day (see page 36).

Nestboxes

Lovebirds like special nesting places. In their native habitat some lovebird species excavate termite nests, which may be located in trees quite high above the ground; terrestrial termite hills are only occasionally used. Lovebirds also sleep and brood in communal weaver's nests and tree hollows. In captivity, these hollows are replaced by a good wooden nestbox.

Nestboxes must be the proper size and built from half-inch or inch-thick plywood with a removable lid. Peach-faced lovebirds, masked lovebirds, and Fischer's lovebirds like boxes measuring 8 × 8 × 8 inches (20 × 20 × 20 cm) or 10 × 6 × 8 inches (25 × 15 × 20 cm). The latter two species can use even larger boxes as they are enthusiastic nest builders. They will fill up a roomy interior with building materials and bring it to the right size. I once had a pair of Fischer's lovebirds that built a roomy nest, about 2 feet 3½ inches (70 cm) in diameter, on a ledge in a corner of the night shelter. There they raised two sets of four young, even though a generous selection of nestboxes was available.

If you use breeding cages, hang the nestboxes outside the cage by one of the doors, so

Housing and Equipment

that you don't lose any inside space. This placement makes inspections easier; you can look at breeding birds without disturbing them and their young. In aviaries, hang the nestboxes as high as possible, with all of them on the same wall.

At breeding time, several couples housed together should have an ample selection of nestboxes; I suggest at least two boxes per couple—all identical to avoid squabbling. Experience has shown that this leads to better breeding results.

Nestboxes provide the birds with an excellent hiding place. Birds will take refuge inside when they hear a sudden noise, spot a predator, or encounter sudden cold or wind.

Nestboxes (above) can easily be made at home. A good size for peach-faced, masked, and Fischer's lovebirds is 8 × 8 × 8 inches (20 × 20 × 20 cm), inside measurements. The entrance hole should have a diameter of 2–3 inches (5–7 cm). The nestbox on the upper left has a double floor; the upper floor is made of sturdy window screening. On the lower floor, there is room for a small water bowl, which can maintain the proper humidity for the nest (see page 24).

They'll stay inside until the coast is clear and conditions are back to normal.

Note that you should *not* supply any nestboxes for birds placed into quarantine after being imported. Nestboxes and sleeping boxes should be avoided for at least 2 weeks because the birds will hide away there even if nothing unusual is happening. As a result, they can't get used to their caretaker, to each other, or to their new environment, and you'll get shy birds that won't breed.

Nestboxes in the night shelter should have a double floor with space for a dish of water between levels. The water keeps the humidity high and the eggs somewhat moist. To get water vapor to the eggs, bore some small holes into the floor on which eggs are deposited, or make the "first floor" out of fine but substantial metal gauze.

Nestboxes in an open run don't need double floors because the boxes are exposed to rain (see page 22). If there is a long dry spell, spray them gently with the garden hose. Naturally, the double-bottomed nestboxes are good in the open also, as they save you the work of spraying.

Sleeping Boxes

As mentioned, you should arrange for winter housing. Where there is a real winter season, you must make arrangements to bring your birds indoors to a draft-free and frost-free berth (see page 24). If your birds are properly banded for identification (see page 62), I recommend separating the sexes during the winter months and giving them large runs to unwind in before the next breeding season, no matter how mild the winter.

You risk too many problems when maintaining birds in their breeding quarters during the winter. If the weather warms up temporarily, for example, they may start breeding prematurely. This is particularly true if you furnish sleeping boxes insulated with sawdust, peat moss, or chaff.

If you do plan to get sleeping boxes, consider the type that is closed on five sides and open at the front, measuring about 4 × 12 × 8 inches (10 × 30 × 20 cm). Put a perch inside, exactly 6 inches (15 cm) from the roof and exactly in the center. You don't want birds to have to perch with the head and shoulders bent and the back and tail hunched.

Provide extra sleeping boxes so your lovebirds won't be forced into fights when they are ready to make a choice for the evening. Each couple will select a sleeping box of its own. Even a young bird that has become independent likes to sleep with one of its brothers or sisters inside a cozy bedroom.

Hang the boxes high in the night shelter of an outdoor aviary to minimize exposure to cold and drafts. With indoor aviaries and other indoor quarters, hang the sleeping boxes high in a corner in as private a space as possible. You want it quiet for the birds.

If you breed a large number of birds, you will probably want to set up separate flights for the newly independent young of the same color mutation. These birds also need sleeping boxes. In that case, you may see two birds pair up in the evening night after night, and you may wonder if they are of different sex, and if they will eventually make a good breeding pair. This may very well be so. I don't mean that at that point they are really into pair formation; they are too young yet (see page 59). I can't be 100 percent sure, but I'd generally say, yes, it looks like a good future match.

However, well before mating time, the birds should be separated in runs for one sex only. If they are properly banded, you will be able to identify the promising couple and bring them back together at the proper time (see page 60). Don't count on it, however; birds that were friendly in their youth may or may not take to each other if they are reintroduced when they reach adulthood.

Suitable Food and Proper Feeding

A bird consumes on average the equivalent of about one-fifth of its body weight per day. That's a great simplification, because the level of activity, environment, time of year, stress, kind of bird, and other factors exert a great influence on the intake of food. Nonetheless, one can assume that lovebirds will consume an average of 1½–2 ounces (45–60 grams) of feed per day. This indicates that they have a solid appetite; if food is denied, they will get sick quickly.

Their main source of food, therefore, must furnish lovebirds all of their nutritional needs, including protein, fats, carbohydrates, vitamins, minerals, and trace elements. No single seed can satisfy these needs entirely, so that the diet of lovebirds needs to be composed of a mix that, in its entirety, supplies all that's needed in adequate amounts.

Lovebirds are big drinkers, too. They need to have drinkable water constantly available, and it needs to be changed several times a day.

It's best to feed and water and otherwise service the needs of lovebirds more or less at the same time each day. They are creatures of habit, and they need to get used to your schedule as well as your appearance. Wear the same clothes each time if possible; consider wearing a laboratory coat. Talk softly to the birds. This may seem peculiar, but it helps keep things calm in the aviary.

The main food source for lovebirds is seeds and grains. They also like green feed, bark, and fruit, although I can't say that they are really enthusiastic about fruit. In the wild, they also eat termites, flies, bugs, and spiders, especially during the breeding season, so that this requirement also needs to be satisfied in captivity (see page 34).

Prepared Feed

Several excellent commercially prepared feeds are on the market. The best known simple diet consists of a good seed mix, dried greens and fruits, soft food, and eggs. This diet works well in practice, and you can feel confident using it for your birds.

One thing to watch for is that seeds are fresh. Check if they sprout: take a sample of about a hundred seeds and place them on a wet paper towel on a plate. Place the plate in a light spot at room temperature. If after 4–6 days more than 60 seeds have sprouted, you know all is well. If fewer seeds sprout, they are probably old and therefore of reduced nutritional value.

Home Mixes

Many bird fanciers use a seed mix made up of 50 percent canary grass seed and 50 percent white millet. In a separate dish they furnish a mix of 40 percent panicum, 40 percent Japanese millet, and 20 percent small sunflower seeds. An excellent supplement on warm summer days is an extra bowl of sprouted sunflower seed.

A good, overall home mix for lovebirds should contain the following:

Canary grass seed: 15 percent
La Plata, finch or white millet: 15 percent
Panicum millet: 10 percent
Japanese millet: 5 percent
Buckwheat: 10 percent
Whole-grain rice (*padi*): 10 percent
Whole-grain or dehulled oats: 10 percent
Broken wheat: 5 percent
Small sunflower seeds: 10 percent
Hemp (if available): 5 percent
Unroasted, shelled peanuts: 5 percent

Suitable Food and Proper Feeding

For a change, you could substitute niger seed, flax seed, milo, or safflower for hemp, rice, or buckwheat.

The first eight seeds in this list furnish about 75 percent carbohydrates. The others furnish about 25 percent fat. The mix also contains all essential amino acids in more than adequate amounts.

Always supplement the seed mix with millet spray, which is also obtainable commercially. Keep it available all year.

During the "vitamin-short" winter months and the breeding season (see page 60), you should also furnish a dish with sprouted seed, especially millet spray, weed seed, grass seed (especially *Poa annua*), and niger and rape seed. You can depend on sprouted seed to replace green feed in winter.

Green Feed and Fruit

"Green feed" includes such items as fresh peas in the pod, spinach, lettuce, endive, mango leaves, strips of kohlrabi, fresh corn, tomatoes, carrot tops, radish, red beet, parsley, dandelion (the whole plant, including the roots!), clover, chickweed (excellent for all pet birds!), watercress, and various garden herbs (including milk thistle and foxtail).

Fruit includes apple, pear, banana, nonpoisonous berries (such as mountain ash and hawthorn), strawberry, raspberry, rose hips, pitted cherries, sweet oranges, grape, tangerine, and kiwi.

Average Composition of Some Commonly Used Seeds for Lovebirds

Seeds	Moisture (%)	Protein (%)	Fat (%)	Fiber (%)	Ca (%)	P (%)	Ash (%)	Carbo-hydrates (%)
Common millet (*Panicum miliaceum*)	9.2	13.1	3.3	9.1	0.03	0.4	4.1	59.7
Spray millet (*Setaria italica*)	12.5	15.0	6.1	11.2	0.03	0.32	6.0	60.1
Canary grass seed (*Phalaris canariensis*)	15.1	13.7	4.1	21.3	0.05	0.55	10.0	56.2
Hullet oats (*Avena sativa*)	10.0	12.1	4.4	12.0	0.09	0.33	3.4	64.3
Niger seed (*Guizotia abyssinica*)	7.0	20.0	43.2	14.3	0.43	0.65	3.5	12
Flax seed (*Linum usitatissimum*)	7.1	24.2	37.0	6.3	0.23	0.66	4.1	20
Sunflower seed (*Helianthus annuus*)	7.1	15.2	28.3	29.1	0.18	0.45	3.2	17.5
Milo (*Andropogon sorghum*)	12.5	12.1	3.6	2.4	0.03	0.27	1.9	69
Safflower (*Carthamus tinctorius*)	7.2	14.3	28.0	31.2	—	—	3.0	16.5

Nuts are important, too. Try some shelled and unshelled peanuts, shelled hazelnuts, shelled and unshelled walnuts, Brazil nuts, fresh acorns, chestnuts, and horse chestnuts.

Green feed and fruit must not have been sprayed with chemicals. Be careful on that score, also, with the fresh branches I suggested you give your birds year-round. Remember, your lovebirds will peel off the bark and eat small pieces or work strips of it into their nest (see page 60).

Fruit intended for lovebirds should be hung on a sturdy nail or hook, where the birds will gladly eat it. If you put it on the floor (where it becomes soiled much more quickly), they sometimes won't touch it.

Branches about 10 inches (25 cm) in length can be from fruit trees, hazel, willow (a real favorite), poplar, plantain, maple, mountain ash, hawthorn, oak, beech, and linden. Lovebirds constantly fuss with these branches, which is excellent therapy for boredom. The gnawing also keeps their beaks in prime condition, and the minerals and trace elements they ingest are extremely beneficial. The gnawing also promotes good elimination.

Once a week, I feed my lovebirds half-ripe unhusked corn, which they especially appreciate during the breeding season. I freeze corncobs during the season, so that I have a whole year's supply. Before I give them to the birds, I let the cobs thaw for 48 hours in a dark spot at room temperature.

Frozen and refrigerated green feed and fruit should never be offered to birds. Everything should first be brought to room temperature, then washed under lukewarm running water and dried somewhat by shaking or blotting with a paper towel.

Insects

As mentioned, lovebirds in the wild hunt termites, flies, worms, and spiders. The birds often catch insects on the wing and swallow them whole.

In captivity, the insects to feed are mealworms, especially during the breeding season. Be sure to kill the mealworms before offering them to the birds. Do this by putting them in an old pair of pantyhose and holding them in boiling water for 3 minutes. The danger in feeding live mealworms is that the birds swallow them whole, so that the still-live worms could try to gnaw their way out of the crop or stomach. This could be fatal for the lovebirds.

I also strongly recommend supplying some white worms and maggots. These are available commercially.

Vitamins

Vitamins are organic constituents that are often not fully supplied by various food sources, even though they are required only in small amounts. Vitamins are essential for various life processes, including reproduction and growth. They are not used for building up tissue or furnishing energy. A vitamin deficiency is called avitaminosis.

Suitable Food and Proper Feeding

Average Composition of Some Commonly Used Vegetables for Lovebirds

Per 100 g consumed food	Pro-tein (g)	Fat (g)	Carbo-hydrates (g)	Na (mg)	K (mg)	Ca (mg)	P (mg)	Fe (IU)	Vitamin A (IU)	Vitamin B₁ (mg)	Vitamin B₂ (mg)	Vitamin C (mg)
Carrot	1.0	0.2	7.3	45	280	35	30	0.7	13,500	70	55	6
Corn salad	1.8	0.4	2.6	4	420	30	50	2.0	7,000	65	80	30
Endive	1.7	0.2	2.0	50	350	50	50	1.4	900	52	120	9
Lettuce	1.2	0.2	1.7	8	220	20	35	0.6	1,500	60	90	10
Parsley	4.4	0.4	9.8	30	1000	240	130	8.0	12,080	140	300	170
Radish	1.0	0.1	3.5	17	255	34	26	1.5	38	33	30	30
Red beet	1.5	0.1	7.6	86	340	30	45	0.9	80	22	40	10
Spinach	2.4	0.4	2.4	60	660	110	48	3.0	8,200	86	240	47

As the name indicates, vitamin A was the first to be discovered. It was followed by a whole series of other vitamins, principally vitamins B, C, D, E, and K. Vitamins B, D, and K are actually a vitamin complex.

Commercial supplements containing multivitamins and, often, essential minerals are available in liquid and powder form. I like the liquid vitamin-mineral mixtures the best because they can be dissolved in the drinking water or sprinkled over fruit and green feed. You can also administer them with a pipette directly into the bird's mouth if this becomes necessary for certain reasons. Vitamin powder, by contract, tends to sink to the bottom of the seed cup. The powder does stick to the seeds somewhat, but the intake remains rather limited because the birds remove the hulls from the seeds.

If you use cod-liver oil as a vitamin supplement, be careful of overdosing. It is an excellent source of vitamins, but an excess could cause an overdose of vitamin A or a deficiency of vitamin E. Also remember that cod-liver oil can spoil rather rapidly once you break the seal on the bottle. Depending on the weather, it should not be kept more than 5–8 months.

In brief, here are some key reasons that vitamins are essential to the lovebird diet.

● Vitamin A is essential for growth, sound skin and feathers, good fertilization, and prevention of night blindness. Good sources are cod-liver oil, corn, wheat germ, green feed, milk, and carrots.

● The vitamin B complex includes some 14 vitamins, most of which can be found in yeast. That is why I often recommend feeding whole-wheat bread to lovebirds, preferably soaked in milk. (Be careful it doesn't turn sour.) Other good sources are cod-liver oil, milk, green feed, and sprouted seed. The B vitamins promote digestion of carbohydrates, promote growth, and prevent anemia.

● Birds can produce vitamin C in their bodies. Further, it is found in various vegetables, oranges, and lemons. Vitamin C promotes resistance to disease and aids in the healing of wounds.

● Birds can also produce vitamin D if they have access to ultraviolet light. They can only utilize vitamin D_3. Vitamin D_2 can't be converted into D_3 in their bodies. Sources of vitamin D can be found in cod-liver oil and milk. Vitamin D is essential for the normal development of bone structure.

● Vitamin E promotes fertility and is found in sprouted seed, especially wheat seed.

Suitable Food and Proper Feeding

• Vitamin K, from the Danish *koagulation* (coagulation) is essential for the proper functioning of the liver and for blood clotting. Good sources are green plant parts, liver, roots, soybeans, and various grains. The bird diet requires only extremely small quantities, and a good menu will satisfy their needs adequately. There in no real need to furnish a vitamin K supplement.

Minerals

Calcium and certain trace minerals are essential for birds. Calcium plays the major role because the birds need it for good bone structure and for manufacturing eggshells. The best limestone should contain phosphoric acid.

The trace elements play a secondary role. Birds need many minerals in extremely small quantities. Without traces of iron, potassium, magnesium, and other minerals, a bird's body can't function properly. You don't have to be overly concerned about trace minerals; there are good supplements available—the multi-vitamin-mineral preparations, which supply all minerals that the birds require.

Also available commercially are mineral blocks and cuttlefish bone, as well as gravel containing oyster shells and charcoal. Oyster shell and charcoal are available in separate packages, and they are essential. Lovebirds regularly go to a lot of effort to find these essential elements on the floor of their cage or aviary. Peach-faced lovebirds look just like little chickens as they scratch the sand and gravel rapidly with both legs. It is a funny sight.

Grit is also an excellent source of various minerals; because of its sharp edges, it does double duty as an aid for the grinding action of the gizzard.

Drinking Water

Drinking water must be clean. It needs to be renewed several times daily, especially during the warm days of summer. At that time, three changes or more are not too many!

To promote easier cleaning, dishes should be made of glass, porcelain, or glazed earthenware. This job is an essential operation.

Many lovebirds, especially the peach-faced lovebird, are extremely susceptible to "sour crop" (candidiasis), which often results from contaminated water. It is a severe, sour-smelling inflammation of the crop. A careful microscopic examination shows colonies of single, oval white cells that lie loosely in chains (hyphae) on the epithelium. Other causes are moldy or spoiled food, bacterial or yeast infections, and the blocked or retarded passage of feed through the digestive tract. Treat the problem with tetracyclines in the drinking water, which gives speedy results. To be safe, consult an avian veterinarian if this problem occurs.

Many lovebirds soak their nesting material in water. There is nothing wrong with this (see page 60), but it does cause problems with debris in the water. Birds are also inclined to throw small twigs, stones, seed, and other dirt into their drinking and bathing water. That is why I like to furnish all water—for both drinking and bathing—in dishes raised on a platform or, at least, on some flagstones or paving tiles. I suggest a platform about 19 inches (50 cm) high but not too big around because otherwise the bird will deposit all sorts of junk next to the dishes and eventually throw some of it into the water.

Care and Management of Lovebirds

The care and management of most species of lovebirds kept in cages and aviaries is not complicated. With a little extra effort, it isn't hard to get quite satisfactory rates of reproduction.

Preventive Care

As soon as you take a new bird home, place it in a good-sized cage that you have prepared ahead of time with the necessary furnishings, feed, and water. In this cage, the new arrival can get its bearings. After several hours, you will notice that the bird starts to take a real interest in its surroundings. If you approach the cage too closely, it may fly up. At any rate, it will at least pay careful attention to you from its perch. Talk to the bird quietly, but don't disturb it any more than necessary. Approach it only to provide fresh feed and water, and move quietly and efficiently. (Don't bother with bath water; see page 26.)

If you obtain several new pairs of birds from the same source and they have been kept together all along, you can keep them together after you bring them home, in a separate indoor aviary. Under any other circumstances house new pairs separately, so that you can see more easily if anything is wrong. You may be able to judge by their actions whether the twosomes you bought are true couples. Then, after several days, you can house all birds together in an indoor aviary, and it won't be long before the birds choose the right partners. Naturally, you should have made arrangements with the seller that you can exchange birds if it seems after some time that they are not true pairs.

Never place newly acquired birds into your existing collection; rather, observe the new arrivals carefully in a cage (see page 16).

Note whether they eat and drink well, don't sleep excessively during the day, react actively when in company, and defend themselves when aggressed upon.

Birds aren't always friendly while feeding. The illustration clearly shows the bird on the right stretching its neck and opening its beak to impress the other bird, which appears properly cowed, judging by its demeanor.

Despite their name, lovebirds sometimes act quite aggressively toward members of their own species. When you add new birds to an existing collection, keep a close eye on them for several days. If there are bullies in the group that don't know when to stop, you will do well to replace them with friendlier specimens. Experience has taught that young birds adapt faster to a change in location than adult birds. Newly imported birds remain scared and suspicious the longest.

Dealing with Lovebirds

Lovebirds are very active birds, both in captivity and in the wild. As soon as dawn breaks, they awake, take a drink, and then go foraging for food. Immediately, they are chirping away. In short, lovebirds are liveliest in the early morning hours.

Care and Management of Lovebirds

Birds groom daily, carefully pulling each feather through the beak while working it thoroughly with the tongue. Worn feathers are removed.

This could create problems for you. If you live in an apartment building, it pays to put the cages in a dark corner and cover them or close the drapes. You want to avoid arousing the neighbors before the sun has risen and the dew is off the grass. Don't keep birds in total darkness, however. Provide a night-light so that they can eat and drink at night (see page 26).

In a garden aviary, hang sleeping boxes in the night shelter. After all birds have entered the shelter in the evening, close the doors if

This is the typical sleeping posture of lovebirds; the head is turned toward the back, the beak is inserted into somewhat fluffed back feathers, and the eyes are closed.

you think the birds will disturb the neighbors at first light the next morning.

By midmorning, lovebirds quiet down considerably; but they become more lively and somewhat noisier in the late afternoon.

Since lovebirds are early feeders, it is clear that they need to be provided with fresh drinking water and fresh feed in the morning. It is desirable to choose a definite time for this, perhaps before you sit down to breakfast. Before you refill the seed cups, blow away all empty seed hulls. Remember that sunflower husks are difficult to blow away. As you blow away the husks, shake the seed cup several times to bring empty husks to the top. This is important, because lovebirds like to hunt through their mix for seeds they are interested in at the moment. In the process, they stir the seed around (and spill them about!), and empty hulls tend to become mixed with the seed.

If you keep many birds in an enclosure, use several seed dishes to prevent fights. As stated earlier, clean the seed containers at least every other day. Dry them well, and fill them only with fresh seed.

Note that the edges of the containers can become quite smeared because this is where the birds sit when they eat. The containers may be smeared inside and out; droppings can also fall into the seed. So check every time whether their utensils need an extra cleaning. Also make sure to keep the waterers and bird baths clean and consistently supplied with fresh water. This is especially important in warm weather (see page 36). Once a week, add several drops of a drinking water disinfectant to the water. (Ask your pet store manager for more details; there are several excellent commercial brands on the market.)

Care and Management of Lovebirds

Management of Caged Lovebirds

Cages are one of several good ways to house lovebirds (see page 18). They must be cleaned and disinfected at least once a week, along with all the attendant utensils.

The cage floor must get a new covering of cage paper, which is covered by a sprinkling of fresh gravel, sand, grit, and charcoal. The perches also should be washed down every time they become soiled by droppings, which usually means every other day. Be sure the perches are completely dry before you replace them in the cage; this prevents rheumatism.

Lovebirds in breeding cages that are in the midst of breeding and caring for their young should be disturbed as little as possible. Nonetheless, you should clean and/or disinfect the seed, water, and bathing utensils every morning and wash the perches whenever necessary. You should clean smudged trellis with a damp cloth.

There are occasions when you will have to take a lovebird into your hand. The birds, however, don't like this and experience the situation as stressful (see page 17). By all means avoid having a bird lie on its back for any length of time while you hold it; generally this makes them so scared that they will lie apparently lame in your hand for several minutes. Before you try to hold an untamed or recently imported bird, be sure first to put on a pair of leather gloves. The bite of a lovebird is strong and painful.

Management of Aviary Lovebirds

Basically, the care, feeding, and management of aviary lovebirds is no different from that needed for caged lovebirds. There is, however, one important point to make: aviary owners often think that cleanup does not need to be as frequent. They may suppose that a good rain shower will clean away much of the droppings. They may have other justifications. These are delusions. Just look carefully at such a person's garden aviary, and you'll see a thick layer of spilled seeds and hulls around the feeding stations. These are ideal hiding places for mold, bacteria, and other disease-causing organisms.

So be sure to give the outdoor aviary the constant care it needs. Perches, floors, and coops need to be inspected at least once each week and cleaned and disinfected whenever they need it. Feed and water utensils and bird baths should preferably be washed daily.

Unpaved garden aviaries need to have the sand floor renewed annually. This should be done in late fall after the end of the breeding season when you may have moved your birds to indoor winter quarters. Remove the top layer about 6 inches (15 cm) down, and replace it with fresh sand. This job is necessary to avoid worm infestations (see page 54).

You can save yourself this tough job if you install a concrete floor with appropriate drainage. You can spray clean it daily with the garden hose and maintain excellent sanitation. Follow up with use of a good disinfectant; several types are readily available and are not dangerous to use:

- Lysol, manufactured by Lehn and Fials Products, Div. of Sterling Drug, Inc.; *dilution*: 4 ounces per gallon of water; an excellent all-purpose disinfectant
- One-Stroke Environ, manufactured by Vestal; *dilution*: ½ ounce per gallon of water; official disinfectant of the U.S. Department of Agriculture
- Chlorox, manufactured by the Chlorox Co.; *dilution*: 6 ounces per gallon of water;

may be corrosive to bare metal; excellent for concrete floors

Playpens and Toys

Several models of playpens are available on the market (see illustration). They are suitable only for tame birds, meaning principally those that have been hand raised.

Before placing your lovebirds in a playpen, be sure that you close the windows and cover them with drapes. Remove poisonous and "prickly" plants, and protect birds from possible contact with hot stoves, open fireplaces, and other potential dangers (see page 00). Remember that however much lovebirds may enjoy the playpen, they are likely to take a tour through the room from time to time and examine the contents up close. Also protect your furniture. If you have something like an antique cupboard that's hard to move, you may have to reconcile yourself to getting beak marks on it or else give up the idea of a playpen altogether.

You can supply all kinds of toys that actively engage the birds. Toys of hardwood are ideal. You can also use natural branches (see page 34), seed bells (provided there is no real bell in it or attached to it), shiny objects (keys, chains, or mirrors), seashells, pieces of raw carrot or potato, dried gourds, and such. Toys of rubber or plastic are dangerous, sometimes deadly. The danger comes from birds ingesting small pieces of rubber. If these are acted upon by digestive enzymes, certain toxins are released that can cause deterioration of the bowel lining and paralysis of the intestinal muscles. The direct result is blockage of the bowel, which causes death.

Nail and Beak Trimming

Nails and beak are generally kept in good, natural trim if lovebirds have regular access to wooden perches of various thickness, fresh tree branches, cuttlefish bone, and similar items. In the garden aviary, provide some rough stones that birds can use as natural nail trimmers.

If despite these precautions you notice a bird developing overly long nails, you must trim them. Catch and hold the bird—but not on its back to avoid stress and shock (see illustration, page 41, for the proper method). Hold the bird up against the light so that you can see the blood vessels outlined against the horn of the nails. You don't want to cut any of these vessels.

Grasp the bird's leg between your index and middle finger while holding the bird in the palm of your hand. Use an extremely

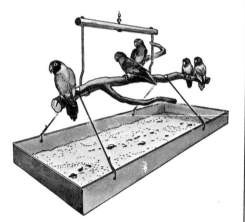

When birds are given the opportunity to fly freely inside the house, it is good to provide a solid perch connected to a sand box. Place bowls of drinking water and seed inside the sand box. This will minimize the time birds spend in your drapes or on your dresser, table, or window sill.

Care and Management of Lovebirds

Here is the proper way to hold a bird when clipping its nails. Hold the head and beak with the thumb and index finger, so that the bird can't bite.

Some hints on nail trimming: the left illustration shows how *not* to do it; the right shows the proper procedure. Be sure not to cut into the part with blood vessels, which can be seen as dark lines through the nail.

sharp pair of nail clippers, and cut just short of the red blood capillaries. Sometimes a capillary grows along with the nail, and you'll get some light bleeding when you cut the nail. So have some styptic cotton at hand to deal with this minor mishap.

Beak trimming is difficult and should be left in the hands of an experienced aviculturist or avian veterinarian.

Dangers for Lovebirds

A number of dangers present themselves when you let lovebirds fly around a room unrestricted: hot stoves, open fireplaces, heaters, open windows, windows without drapes, electrical appliances, electrical cords, doors that can blow shut, and many others. Furthermore, birds can catch their nails on all sorts of furnishings, such as drapes, carpets, pillows, and cloth covers. Before you give birds free flight of the house, ask yourself first which potential dangers need to be dealt with.

Another type of risk is presented by house-plants. Don't take any chances, and remove all houseplants from the area where birds are to fly loose. For the record, here are a few plants known to be poisonous to birds: autumn crocus, azalea, balsam pear, bird of paradise, boxwood, caladium, castor bean, chalice vine, coral plant, daffodil, *Datura* berries, *Dieffenbachia*, eggplant (except for the fruit), taro or elephant's ear, hyacinth, hydrangea, Japanese yew, Java beans, lantana, lily of the valley, narcissus, all varieties of nightshade, oleander, philodendron etc.

Birds that are allowed to fly freely through the house can face all sorts of dangers, especially in the kitchen. An electric stove can cause serious burns.

If Your Lovebirds Get Sick

As a bird fancier, it is important to know what a healthy lovebird looks like. In case of any deviations, you can then promptly take note and take action. Experience is important in this respect. You can be a born bird lover, but you still need years of experience to be a bird expert, and even a bird expert doesn't hesitate to ask advice from an avian veterinarian. If no one with that specialty is available in your immediate neighborhood, write the Association of Avian Veterinarians, P.O. Box 299, East Northport, N.Y. 11731; or telephone (516) 757-6320. No doubt they will be able to put you in touch with a specialized veterinarian.

Be Alert to Unusual Behavior

When a lovebird gets sick, you quickly notice an end to its usual smooth feathering, its chatter, its activity, and its clear-eyed look. The bird seems to withdraw completely. Its feathers look ruffled, and the patient sits with eyes closed, asleep a lot of the time. It tends to lose its natural flight response. It loses interest in its environment. It loses its appetite (*anorexia*) or persists in staying at the feeding cup (*polyphagia*). The gloss disappears from the feathers, and the eyes look sleepy.

Keep an eye on the droppings. These may change color and may be loose, probably because the patient suddenly starts drinking more than normal. If, however, you notice that the amount of droppings is noticeably less than usual, also keep close watch on the bird. It can be a sign that it isn't eating. That's important to know, because a bird must continue to eat, no matter what. If necessary, furnish its favorite food.

If you notice a lot of tail bobbing in a bird or if it seems to hang rather than sit on its perch, it is also time you make a close check. Listen for difficulty in breathing and signs of sneezing or "clicking"; watch for incessant scratching, and be alert for a sudden halt in vocalization. All these can be signs that a bird is becoming ill.

The experienced bird fancier can see at a glance if something is wrong with a bird. That's an advantage. The inexperienced bird lover tends to become aware of problems much more slowly and often too late. That is why it is of utmost importance to check on the birds every day—and with a careful eye. Don't pass over a single bird. Become aware of any deviation in the looks or activities of the birds, and be ready to respond quickly.

Be sure to look at the droppings in your daily check. As I mentioned, droppings can tell us a great deal about the body functions of the birds. The droppings of almost all parrots (the exceptions are the lories) are grayish white, and they shouldn't be too thin. Thin, colorless droppings or any deviation in color points to possible intestinal troubles or other types of illness.

Whenever you notice any signs of illness, take action *immediately*! Don't delay. Don't wait to see if the symptoms you noticed get worse. Don't think that this might be a common variation that could go away. Nothing unusual should be ignored. Symptoms don't appear for no reason, and much as you might wish, they don't just go away. If you delay action, you run every chance that the illness will get worse quickly and that even the best countermeasures you might take will be too late.

What should you do? First of all, you should do some careful and systematic research to discover the nature of the disease—

If Your Lovebirds Get Sick

to make a correct diagnosis. It bears repeating that making a correct diagnosis is extremely difficult. You are not a veterinarian and don't have the required know-how to treat sick birds. The most experienced bird fancier often has trouble determining the nature of an illness, and even an avian veterinarian can't do this with a cursory examination. Often, a veterinarian needs to make a detailed and technical analysis to determine from which sickness a bird is suffering.

In some cases, however, the symptoms are clear, especially if you have had previous experience with the same illness. In other cases, you will be fortunate enough to find a series of symptoms listed in a book (see bibliography, page 80) that match those of your bird, or you may find a good lead on where else to look for help.

At other times, it is not so easy. You will have to use your best judgment. Take the measures you hope will cure your patient, or seek the advice of an avian veterinarian.

In all cases of illness, I believe, it is worthwhile to give the problem your best shot. Even a bird that's cheap to replace loves life and should be saved from death. If you don't want to take the trouble to save its life, you ought to collect bird pictures, not live birds.

Every attempt at least teaches you something new. If you take the necessary precautions, you will not cause any harm by making judicious use of medications. In most cases, you also will enjoy the sweet taste of success. You will take pride in releasing a bird into your aviary that, at one point, seemed marked for death.

Start by gently taking the bird showing symptoms out of the cage or aviary. Now give it a thorough and detailed examination.

Blow aside the feathers around the cloaca. Notice whether the area around the cloaca is moist and sticky. If so, this points to a digestive problem or a bacterial infection. In many cases like this the skin around the cloaca and on the belly is red and inflamed.

Wet nostrils and a labored, squeaky respiration point to colds. A gasping beak points to aspergillosis. See if the eyes have an inflamed rim. Carefully palpate legs and wings to see if they are normal. Look under the wings; blow aside some feathers there, and look sharply to see if there are any parasites. You may have to use a magnifying glass. Examine the entire body for wounds or tumors.

In females, carefully palpate the rear end (cloaca) of the bird to be sure you're not dealing with egg binding.

Think back as to possible causes of trouble. Have you been furnishing the right feed? Could there be a shortage of protein, vitamins, or minerals? Was the drinking water dirty or impure, so that this could be a cause of the problem? Was the bird exposed to drafts, or did it experience a sudden, large change in temperature, leading to a cold? Could it be a case of poisoning caused by spoiled feed?

In short, consider every possible cause and try to discover every likely symptom. Once you are on the right track, it is always much easier to find the right remedy.

The Hospital Cage

On completing your examination, place the bird in a warm, separate spot, preferably in a special hospital cage. You want to keep the patient apart to keep from infecting the other birds. I recommend you get a cage designed to care for sick birds; sick people get hospital

If Your Lovebirds Get Sick

beds, and sick birds should get hospital cages. I like those with a glass front, which allows me to keep a close watch on my patient. The cage should have special heat lamps, which you should adjust to the right temperature.

If you don't have a separate hospital cage, any small cage will do. Cover the cage with a piece of cloth, leaving a small opening only in front. This allows the bird to sit in peace. If sunlight is available, turn the cage so that some light will shine in. You can help keep the bird warm with a small heat lamp or infrared light.

A bird in a hospital cage is easier to observe. Keep doing so, with an eye out for symptoms that you may have missed in your initial examination. Keep a close watch on the droppings as a barometer of how the sick bird is doing.

If you act quickly and the bird isn't too sick, merely keeping it separated in a hospital cage may cure it. The rest and peace, at any rate, promote natural healing.

At first, keep the temperature (day *and* night) in the hospital cage between 90 and 95°F (33 and 35°C). You need a thermometer inside the cage to watch this closely. If the temperature goes up too high, you can turn off one of the heat lamps or increase the ventilation.

Hospital cages have ventilation slots on the underside that let in fresh air. The incoming air can be heated with the heat lamps. Warm air rises and leaves the cage through ventilation slots in the top.

Never close all the ventilation slots, for your patient needs fresh air at all times. At least one slot on the top and one on the bottom should be kept open.

Furnish your patient the same feed you've been providing. Make sure that it eats. If the bird resumes its normal feeding pattern, you usually won't need to furnish any medication. As the bird recovers, slowly lower the heat. After several days, you can turn off all the heat lamps, and if all stays well for another few days, you can return the bird to its old cage or aviary.

Now, let's cover some specific symptoms you will need for a good diagnosis.

Missing Feathers

Healthy feathers lie tightly against the bird's body. You will notice this especially in a bird that just completed a molt and has a whole new suit of feathers. Lovebirds spend a lot of effort to maintain their appearance. Many times each day they groom their feathers with their beak.

It isn't hard, therefore, to notice if any feathers are missing. This can have a natural cause, for example, during molt. It can also be a sign of trouble, indicating some type of illness.

Problematic feather loss can be caused by improper feeding, a drafty environment, parasites, infections, metabolic and hereditary disorders, and other problems. If you notice any feather loss, first investigate the cause.

If your bird has any broken or split feathers, remove these or trim them back to keep the bird or its cage mates from picking at the problem. Such problems often develop when moving birds from one home to another, when catching a bird, or in fights with other birds.

In flight lovebirds have a remarkable speed and dexterity. Top: Nyasa lovebird. Bottom: black-cheeked lovebird.

44

If Your Lovebirds Get Sick

If feathers bleed, apply some Morsel solution or styptic powder using a cotton-tipped applicator or your bare finger. Styptic powder burns the mouth, so be especially careful if you need to apply it near the beak. Bleeding in feathers that are still growing can be caused by catching maneuvers, fights, tight quarters, and excessive trimming.

Under no circumstances should you leave feathers lying on the bottom of the cage or the floor of the aviary. Loose feathers invite trouble because birds will tend to get into the habit of picking at them.

Feather Picking

Some birds have the nasty habit of picking their own feathers, especially large parrots, like macaws and African grays. In the worst cases, a bird may pick itself completely bald, except for some sturdy wing and tail feathers and those on the top of the head that it can't reach with its beak. Lovebirds can also pick other lovebirds' feathers; they may even pluck their young.

Many cases of feather picking can't be explained. You can prevent most cases, however, and cure them as well by giving birds something to do. To begin with, put fresh branches into their cage every day, complete with leaves. They love to gnaw on them. Also, see to it that there is enough light in the cage, that it isn't too small or overstocked, that the temperature and humidity are right, and that each bird can take a bath every day.

The page opposite presents various color mutations of the peach-faced lovebird. Above, left: red pied. Above, right: lutino (golden cherry). Below, left: pastel blue. Below, right: albino.

Birds should be able to bathe any time of day, except in outside aviaries, where you should remove the bath water after 4 p.m. to allow the birds to go to sleep dry and not exposed to chills.

Stress can be a major cause of feather picking (page 17). Another is insufficient rest. I have noticed that practically all cage birds require at least 10–12 hours of sleep.

Birds that persist in the "bad habit" can be given an "Elizabethan collar." They will get used to the device within a few days, although there are cases in which the bird doesn't want to have anything to do with it and keeps trying hard to remove the collar. If this goes on for several days, give in. Often the bird is cured of the habit by then, because it was trying so intensively to remove the collar that it totally forgot about picking feathers.

Bald Spots

Lovebirds seldom are infested with external parasites, but infestations can happen, particularly with red mites (*Dermanyssus gallinae*). I know of cases started by sparrows that dropped their feathers while roosting on the roof of an aviary. Newly imported lovebirds also can suffer from a range of parasites; you will be able to spot them by their "moth-eaten" feathers and bald spots.

The large red mite (about 1 mm long) lives from blood that it sucks from the birds. Its life cycle generally doesn't exceed 3 weeks. In that time, it lays its eggs in crevices and cracks. In a warm and somewhat humid environment, these eggs hatch in 48–72 hours, spend several days as larvae, and develop into adults thereafter.

Mites attack birds of all ages. Some mites specialize in certain bird species; some even attack humans. The red mite characteristically is active only at night, and it is then that it bothers the birds. During the day the mites withdraw to their crevices and cracks. You can also find them under and behind cages, as well as in nestboxes and other hiding places.

Because mites are active at night, they can cause your lovebirds a lot of discomfort. They don't give the birds a moment of rest while they suck their fill of blood. Before their meal, the mites are gray; afterward they show their typical red coloration.

Infested birds often don't sleep at all during the night and therefore sleep a lot during the day. Brooding birds can't stand staying on the nest if they suffer from mites, and infested young tend to leave the nest earlier than normal, often in a weak and poorly feathered condition.

Mites tend to multiply twice as fast during warm, humid weather. Large hordes can attack your sleeping birds, resulting in anemia, weakness, and even death. If you're trying to breed lovebirds in infested aviaries, you may just as well give up. The mites tend to multiply to such an extent that you can stick a knife in any crack in the wood and come up with a blood-stained blade.

Many insecticides are effective against the red mite. Most of them contain pyrethrin, made from the pyrethrun flower, a chrysanthemum. Pyrethrin is harmless to birds. It is usually mixed with other, equally harmless materials that activate pyrethrin so that it does its job better.

With a parasite infestation, you can't take half-measures. Put your birds in a temporary clean cage or aviary, as far away from the infested area as possible. Treat all nestboxes and sleeping boxes with boiling water. Treat all joints and crevices with creosote or boiling water, using a small brush. Brush insecticide powder into all crevices, joints, cracks, and openings. Clean off all perches and other furniture, and rinse them with boiling water. Repeat this entire procedure after about 5 days and again after another week.

Meanwhile, treat your birds with pyrethrin (or carbaryl), with special attention to the neck, the area around the cloaca, and under the wings. Don't put them back into their old quarters before everything there is completely dry.

You often can't tell if you've been invaded by red mites, especially if you haven't had years of experience in the field. Look for these signs of infestation: weakness and listlessness in otherwise healthy birds; constant searching with beaks through the feathers; restlessness at night; interruption of breeding; and neglect of the young.

Confirm your suspicions of red mite infestation by catching one of your birds late in the evening and examining it under a strong light. If there is an infestation, you will be able to see the red mites run among the feathers and over your hand.

If you keep birds in small cages, hang a white cloth over the cages at night. If you have an infestation, you will be able to see the mites on the cloth the next morning. You can get rid of a good part of the infestation by putting the cloth in boiling water to kill the mites.

As I mentioned, lovebirds seldom become infested with other types of parasites, such as lice, fleas, or ticks, all of which can be seen with the naked eye. Wild-caught and imported birds, however, often have ticks.

Ticks are gray and, like mites, belong to

the arachnids. Ticks tend to let themselves drop off as soon as they have sucked their fill of blood. Once they digest their meal, they look for a new host.

Don't worry if you can't tell a tick from a louse or flea. All three can be combated with pyrethrin or carbaryl.

Repeat the treatment after several days to be sure you eliminate developing life stages—the young adults, the larvae, and the eggs (which can be seen as tiny, white clusters, called "nits").

French Molt

Like other members of the psittacidae family, young lovebirds can be affected by French molt. Victims of this malady are commonly known as runners or creepers because they have retarded growth and poor feathering, so that they cannot fly. The remaining primary flight and tail feathers are short and undeveloped or are missing entirely. The rest of the plumage is thin, especially on the breast.

For the rest, there are no obvious symptoms. You don't notice any loss in vitality. Creepers are active and alert and usually stay mobile by climbing around in their cages.

A microscopic examination of young feathers reveals that the follicle and quill have capillaries (small blood vessels) with extremely weak walls. The exact cause of the problem is unknown and a virus (papovavirus) is suspected but not definitely comfirmed, despite considerable research.

At this time (1986), no good remedy has been found, even though scientists around the world are busy looking for one. This is a great pity, because many birds will never get a normal complement of feathers.

It goes without saying that creepers are not to be used for breeding. If you keep them around, feed them a varied diet rich in protein at all times of the year.

Eye Disease

Lovebirds can be subject to several types of eye infections. In most cases, the problem results from complications of colds and resulting side infections caused by bacteria or viruses. Other possible causes are a deficiency in vitamin A or the use of aerosol sprays or dusty seed that irritates the eye.

A bird that has caught a cold in one or both eyes will close the affected eyes. Eyes are teary, and the edges are inflamed.

Bacterial infections often start as a result of dirty perches. The bird picks up the infection by wiping its beak along the dirty perch. Another common cause is shipment of a large consignment in a small box, so look for trouble in recently imported birds. This type of infection causes the edges of the eye to be heavily inflamed—generally just *one* eye.

Place the patient in a warm environment, preferably in a hospital cage. Rinse the eyes with 5 percent boric acid, or apply an antibiotic ophthalmic ointment twice or three times daily (Neosporin or Neopolycin are good commercial products). A few days of treatment are usually sufficient to assure a speedy recovery. It can't hurt to consult an avian veterinarian about the problem.

Knemidokoptes mites (see Scaly Face, page 56) can also indirectly irritate eyelids and eyes when the typical scabs occur around the eye and eyelid. Treat the scabs with penicillin ointment, and also treat the edges of the eye.

If there are wartlike little bumps on the lid, there may be a vitamin A deficiency, pointing to the need to drastically alter the diet. At any rate, separate a sick bird with these little warts because they can be a symptom of psittacine pox. This disease requires help from an avian veterinarian.

Serious cases of eye infection can lead to partial or complete blindness in one or both eyes. This result is generally preceded by heavy tearing, after which the pupil turns milky white.

Birds that become partially or totally blind can be kept alive in a small cage. In the beginning, place food and water on the floor of the cage, preferably in a shallow earthenware dish. It takes a while for the blind bird to find its feed and water, although the learning process goes faster for a bird that has been kept in a cage all along, compared with an aviary bird.

Fractures

Fractures of the leg or wing can be avoided by handling birds gently and protecting them from barking dogs and prowling cats. If accidents do happen, consult an avian veterinarian, especially if you are a beginning aviculturist.

If you treat a broken leg yourself, line up the severed sections and splint the fracture with a couple of thin sticks (wooden matches) on each side of the leg. Keep the splint in place by winding gauze around it and taping it with a piece of surgical tape. Wind the gauze tightly; you want to restrict the movement of the broken leg as much as possible.

Any bandage allows some movement. To avoid this as much as possible, I prefer an alternate method. I wrap the fractured leg with small strips of gauze that were previously treated in a thin preparation of plaster of Paris. First, wrap the leg twice, line up the leg properly, and wait until the plaster sets. Then, wrap another couple of strips around the fracture.

It is harder to heal fractures occurring close to the body of the bird, and it may be especially useful to use the gauze-plus-plaster method in these cases. Better yet, these tricky fractures require the skills of an avian veterinarian.

Sometimes a torn muscle is mistaken for a broken leg. This condition can occur when a bird makes desperate movements to free itself when caught in wire mesh, possibly because of overly long nails. Torn muscles are difficult to heal. You can try to immobilize the affected leg with a bandage and keep it on while nature takes its course.

Birds with a leg injury should be kept in a hospital cage without perches until the healing process is complete. Cover the cage bottom with peat moss. Darken the cage partially, and place it in a quiet location so that the injured bird will move as little as possible. Be sure that the diet contains an adequate amount of vitamins and minerals.

Broken, drooping wings can best be bandaged with gauze. Cut a slit into the gauze, and put the folded wing through the slit. Then wrap gauze around the body and secure it to a leg to keep it from sliding off. Make sure the bandage is tight without pinching the bird.

Wing fractures also require placement of the patient in a dark, quiet spot for several weeks. Use a cage without perches that is low enough to prevent the bird from flying. Although the bird will get used to the treated leg or wing, it is sometimes necessary for the patient to wear an Elizabethan collar. This prevents the bird from picking the treated injury.

Let me emphasize once again that setting a broken wing is a difficult task, and it's better to entrust it to a vet. The treatment I suggested is likely to keep the wing in a proper position, but the bird may not be able to fly afterward.

Egg Binding

When lovebirds are housed and fed properly, egg binding will be a rarity. Egg binding means that the affected bird can't lay an egg that's ready to come out. The affected female looks sick, sits hunched up, moves little, and is easy to catch by hand in most cases. If you feel its abdomen, you quickly notice the trouble—the stuck egg.

In the normal course of events, an egg spends no more than 24 hours in the cloaca and the wide section of the ovary leading to the cloaca. When it is ready, the muscles in the lowest part of the ovary push it into the cloaca, where it usually remains only a short time before it is pushed entirely out of the body.

The muscles involved can fail to function properly as a result of a cold, an infection, or a vitamin deficiency. The affected bird will try valiantly to lay the egg, but in vain.

Another form of egg binding can result from shell-less or thin-shelled eggs (wind eggs). This condition can be caused by some malfunction in the deposit of calcium on the egg or by a calcium shortage. The weak or absent shell tends to cause the egg to get stuck because the muscles in the ovary and cloaca can't get a good grip on the soft mass.

Egg binding is entirely preventable under normal situations. Clearly, vitamin shortage

Be quick to act if you spot a bird looking like the one in this drawing—huddled on the floor with fluffed-up feathers and eyes closed. Without a doubt, you have a sick bird on your hands.

must be prevented. Be sure that while the bird is breeding it has an ample supply of green feed and sprouted seed.

To prevent wind eggs, be sure that your birds have enough calcium, particularly calcium phosphate. Commercial bird grit contains the key minerals, including calcium, so you really don't have to do more than see to it that there is always plenty of grit in the cage or aviary.

A further caution to prevent egg binding is not to start breeding too early in the breeding season. The temperature and humidity are probably not ideal so early. Also, never, ever breed females that are too young. Immature birds are extremely likely candidates for egg binding.

Egg binding also is entirely curable, provided you act fast enough. First, use a plastic

If Your Lovebirds Get Sick

dropper to put a few drops of warm mineral oil in the cloaca, so that the egg can be laid more easily. Don't use such an "artificially laid" egg for breeding. Second, transfer your patient to a hospital cage and raise the temperature to about 90°F (33°C) with an infrared lamp. Warmth and rest should allow your patient to recover. I recommend, however, that you consult a veterinarian as soon as you notice any sign of egg binding.

Egg Pecking

Lovebirds sometimes peck at eggs lying in the nest. Act immediately, and remove the culprit from the cage or aviary. There is no known cause for egg pecking, but I am sure that the chance of it occurring is very small if you provide proper feeding, housing, and "entertainment."

Colds

Respiratory difficulties can come about through all kinds of problems: drafts, low temperatures, exposure to various bacteria, fungi, and viruses, vitamin A deficiency, and stress (see page 17). You will notice that the patient has a rapid, audible respiration. The beak will be open, and the tail bobs. The bird will sneeze, cough, and have a nasal discharge and won't eat. Often you will find the patient sitting quietly in a corner with ruffled feathers.

Immediately place the patient in a warm environment and minimize stress. If there is a discharge from the nostrils, remove it carefully with a cotton ball. Use a vaporizer to spray a fine, warm mist of water into the cage to soothe and moisturize the inflamed lining of the respiratory tract. A standard vaporizer available at the drugstore is fine. In any case,

consult an avian veterinarian. Check if housing, location, feeding, and temperature are up to standard.

Diarrhea

Intestinal upsets in lovebirds can be caused by a number of factors. One is poor food—poorly selected or in poor condition because of spoilage or poison. Other possible causes are obesity, respiratory or intestinal infection, excessive heat, or an excess of protein. Many bacterial and viral infections cause intestinal disturbances along with other symptoms.

Outward symptoms of impaired intestinal function are listlessness, "hunching," and diarrhea. A serious case is manifested when a bird will no longer rest on the perches and takes to the floor. It will sit in a corner, head under its wings. The bird tends to drink quite a bit but will have little appetite. The droppings are watery.

I think it best to call an avian veterinarian for intestinal disturbances. Meanwhile, you can try home remedies. Personally, I have had good success with chamomile tea. You may also give the patient boiled rice, oat flakes, and spray millet.

Put the sick bird in a hospital cage, with the temperature raised to about 90°F (33°C) using an infrared lamp. Together with the antibiotics prescribed by the veterinarian, quiet and warmth will help the patient recover quickly.

Intestinal disturbances can also occur if your aviary is poorly ventilated and the weather turns quite warm. Cold weather also can be a cause. Extremes in temperature are a threat to the health of your birds.

Cold water is a special problem, particularly if your drinking dishes freeze in cold weather and your birds have had to do without

If Your Lovebirds Get Sick

water for several hours. Lovebirds, in contrast to other parrots, drink a lot of water. So don't give parched birds cold water straight from the faucet. They will drink too much of it, leading to possible intestinal problems. Instead, provide it lukewarm, which should be the rule in winter.

Poisoning, light or heavy, can cause intestinal problems. Birds can be poisoned by spoiled feed or by poisonous substances. Be especially careful to avoid exposure to DDT and lindane in insecticides and other chemical sprays.

If you suspect your lovebirds have been poisoned, place them in a warm place and furnish fresh green feed and clean drinking water in which you have dissolved a little bicarbonate of soda. Another good purge is fresh milk or a few drops of Pepto-Bismol. Never provide bicarbonate of soda for more than 3 days running, and always in low concentrations, such as 1 gram in a full glass of water.

A special type of poisoning occurs when birds get an excessive amount of protein, especially during the breeding season. The same condition can be brought on by an excess of egg feed and soft feed. Often, the breeder simply forgets that egg feed should be provided in addition to, not instead of, the usual feed. Affected birds suddenly show all the typical symptoms of poisoning; they seem dull and sleepy, they have trouble breathing, and they cease flying. Often they have a severe diarrhea and can quickly die.

Be aware that diarrhea can be a symptom of a great number of avian diseases, but you don't have to suspect serious disease problems if you notice signs of diarrhea. If there are no other symptoms pointing to a specific illness, it can simply be a question of ordinary indigestion. For such cases, provide rice water instead of the usual drinking water, or use Norit. Dissolve a tablet of Norit in a tablespoon of water, and give the patient one or two drops in the beak, using a feeding syringe or a medical, plastic dropper.

A watery discharge isn't always diarrhea. Lovebirds may react this way from fear, from being picked up by hand, or even from being observed too closely.

Still, if you notice diarrhea, the safest response is to consult an avian veterinarian.

Obesity

Birds that lack exercise because their cage is too small or because they haven't enough toys to keep them occupied may become fat. Birds that do not receive proper nutrition also are liable to fall victim to obesity.

Getting fat is, however, a very slow process. The owner must be alert and watch carefully for the first signs of obesity. When the bird can barely sit on its perch, things have already gone too far. The bird might sit on the bottom of its cage, lethargic and panting heavily. The contours of its body become blurred, heavy, and cylindrical, and the skin appears yellowish when the feathers on the breast or abdomen are blown apart. This is the fat shining through the skin.

Birds suffering from obesity live much shorter lives than those that have plenty of exercise and lively interests. The obese bird has difficulty molting and just sits, looking thoroughly bored.

The first thing is to give the birds plenty of exercise. Caged lovebirds must be released daily in a secure area and allowed to fly freely for at least an hour. Inside the cage or (small) aviary, birds must have even more exercise. Consider housing them in larger cages or placing perches further apart. Hang some strong sisal ropes in the cage and a few bunches of spray millet or weed seeds. Lovebirds love to play with these.

Next, improve the birds' nutrition (strictly by the book if necessary), and provide lots of well-washed greens or fruit free of chemicals. Definitely do not provide food with a high protein or fat content. Do not work from the assumption, "My bird is fat, so if I don't feed it for a few days it will be all right again." The bird must be fed, but with the right kind of food. It will perish, however fat it might be, if it receives no nourishment.

Goiter

Goiter, or enlargement of the thyroid gland, is particularly common among lovebirds, cockatiels, Australian grass parakeets (rosellas, Bourks, and others), and budgerigars.

Fortunately, this disorder no longer occurs frequently because commercial cage sand is often treated with iodine. The problem is still common, however, in areas where drinking water is deficient in iodine.

Usually goiter is not recognized by an external swelling. The growth, pressing against crop and windpipe, is internal. Clearly, any exertion such as flying and running will make the affected bird breathless very quickly. Breathing heavily, it will drop to the ground, often with widespread wings and pendulous crop and neck. It also might make a high-pitched squeak or wheezing sound with each breath.

In order to breathe more easily, the bird often will rest its beak against the bars of the cage or on a parallel perch or tree branch. If you fail to act immediately the disease will worsen. The bird might start to walk in circles—an indication of cerebral infection. Sudden death might then follow due to suffocation, heart failure, or weakness due to insufficient intake of food.

In the case of a serious thyroid disorder, give the bird iodine-glycerine. The proper mixture for lovebirds is one part tincture of iodine to five parts of glycerine. As an alternative, a mixture consisting of nine parts paraffin oil to one part iodine-glycerine, administered with a plastic dropper in a corner of the beak intermittently over a period of 3 days usually works wonders. If the condition persists, see your avian veterinarian.

Worms

If you keep an outdoor aviary, it is hard to escape worm infestations. The worms are brought in by wild birds that perch on the aviary and let their droppings fall inside.

Roundworms (*Ascaris*) start as long, white larvae that grow to adulthood in the intestines of birds that swallow them. The adults, in turn, lay eggs that exit from the bird's body in the droppings.

Infested birds quickly lose weight, develop poor feathering, and suffer from diarrhea or constipation. To confirm a parasite infestation, take a stool sample to your avian veterinarian, who is likely to prescibe piperazine or levamisole.

The best prevention is first-rate hygiene and sanitation. For one thing, regularly spray clean the aviary floor if it is made of concrete.

Threadworms (*Capillaria*) start as round, threadlike parasites that attain adulthood in the crop or small intestine of the bird. Adult

If Your Lovebirds Get Sick

worms lay eggs that leave the bird's body in the droppings.

Signs of infestation include diarrhea and weight loss. Confirm the problem by having a stool sample analyzed. The veterinarian is likely to prescribe piperazine or levamisole. Prevention depends on excellent hygiene and sanitation.

Coccidia are microscopic protozoan parasites, which occur infrequently in lovebirds. They are spread in the droppings, consumed by the bird, and mature in the intestines. Ordinarily, they pose no danger to lovebirds. Birds can be infested for a long time before anyone notices. However, consult an avian veterinarian if you notice a gradually decreased appetite, typically coupled with weight loss and loose droppings that may be somewhat bloody. These symptoms could signal a case of coccidiosis. If confirmed, sulfa drugs may be helpful. It is important to have recently imported birds checked for coccidiosis. Prevention depends on good hygiene and sanitation.

E. coli Infections

Infections with *Escherichia coli*, gram-negative bacteria generally known as *E. coli*, can pose serious problems for lovebirds. *E. coli* principally infect humans, but birds are not immune.

Don't let anyone tell you that *E. coli* are normal residents of the bird's intestines. They can also easily spread to the lungs, liver, and heart and can lead to a speedy death.

The best preventive is good personal hygiene. Wash your hands before you move birds, prepare feed, inspect nests, and carry out other activities with your birds. Prevent fecal contamination, and avoid spoiled food,

dirty water, dirty perches, dirty nest boxes, dirty floors in cages and aviaries, and other sources of contamination.

Treatment consists of three to four drops Kaopectate or Pepto-Bismol every 4 hours. Administer with a plastic medicine dropper. This will soothe and coat the inflamed digestive tract. Seek veterinary assistance if rapid improvement is not observed within 24 hours; there are a number of antibiotics that can provide relief, but they can be obtained only through a veterinarian.

Molt

Many fanciers say that molt is a "healthy disease." This means, of course, that molt is no disease at all, even if during molt birds show symptoms reminiscent of a disease, for example a slight elevation in body temperature.

Molt is no mystery. It is the annual renewing of the bird's worn feathers. The old feathers fall out, and in a relatively short time new feathers grow in. These will have to last the bird until another year is up.

Be aware that the period of molt makes high demands on the bird's body. First of all, the bird loses heat when its feathers fall out. Second, a large amount of energy is required to support a completely new growth of feathers in a relatively short time.

Molting, in a sense, starts with nestlings, who replace their down with "real" feathers. These are their "youth feathers," which remain for 3 or 4 months. Then the first real molt occurs, and the young bird gets its first adult plumage.

In adult birds, molt more or less signals the close of the breeding season. The season starts in the early spring with mating and brooding. Then follows a rest period, after which the bird gets ready for the next season. Molt is part of that preparation. It is initiated by the shorter periods of daylight in fall, which trigger an increase in hormone activity. The feathers lose their elasticity, and they drop out—fortunately not all at once. Nature has arranged it so that a bird never loses so many flight feathers that it cannot fly. First a few flight feathers drop. These are replaced by new ones before further flight feathers fall out to be replaced in their turn. The loss of any type of feather is balanced more or less by the replacement of the same type of feather, so that a lovebird is never bald during molt.

The period of molt requires extra care from you. First, take special precautions against having your lovebirds catch a cold. Second, make sure they have access to a protein-rich diet with plenty of vitamins (especially vitamins A and D), minerals (calcium and cuttlefish bone), and a rich assortment of green feed. Allow your birds as much rest as possible. If you have indoor aviaries and cages, spray your birds with water at room temperature in the morning, or give them an opportunity to bathe. Bathwater should also be furnished at room temperature.

With this type of care, molt will go quickly and smoothly, especially if you keep birds in an outside aviary. The freedom of movement helps things along.

Abnormal molt can occur from such problems as sudden changes in temperature, changes in light periods, and repeated stress or shock. Feather regrowth is normally complete in 6–8 weeks. If after that time the new feathers have not come in yet, there may be a problem with hormone imbalance. Be sure to consult an avian veterinarian. Then check the diet, housing, and hours of light provided, and watch for fights between birds. The veterinarian will check whether the thyroid gland is functioning properly and whether a dietary supplement would help.

Scaly Face

Scaly face is caused by mites (*Knemidokoptes pilae*). These attack the skin area around the eyes and beak and also the legs and toes in serious cases. These insect like parasites burrow passages in the top layers of the skin, where they lay their eggs. If left untreated, the rough scales that result steadily grow worse and serious deformities of the beak can occur. The condition spreads from one bird to another if you don't take action.

The crusty scales can be treated with Vaseline or glycerine. You can also use mineral oil, but be careful to daub it on the infected area only and don't drip oil on the feathers. In serious cases, consult an avian veterinarian, who will treat the affected area with Eurax Cream or with Ivermectic (Equalan), an injectible medication.

Remove any scaly scabs that fall off as quickly as possible, and burn them if you can. Then avoid further spreading by cleaning the cage, perches, sleeping boxes, and nestboxes. Scaly face is not a dangerous infection, but it is a troublesome one that merits great care to be sure it is completely eradicated.

Frozen Toes

Cold winter days pose the possibility of frozen toes. This may occur when lovebirds hang on the wire mesh too long, which they tend to do if they are suddenly disturbed. Perches that are too thin may also cause problems because the lovebirds' toes are partially bare (not covered by feathers). Obviously, you need to replace the perches in such cases. If you use sleeping boxes cover the bottom with a warm layer of peat moss.

If this problem strikes, there's not much you can do, much as I hate to say this. In fact, you do more harm than good. The best course is to consult a veterinarian, who may prescribe a salve.

The frozen part dries out and drops off without any apparent harm to the bird. Be sure that no infections occur at that point. At the first sign, treat the wound immediately with noncaustic iodine.

Psittacosis

Psittacosis is the same illness in parrots and parakeets that is called ornithosis in other species of birds. It occurs only rarely in lovebirds.

This serious disease is caused by an obligate intracellular parasite, *Chlamydia psittaci*, distinguished from all other microorganisms by a unique growth cycle. It occurs especially in dirty breeding operations and can be brought in by imported birds, especially smuggled birds. Be suspicious of dirty-looking birds. They may look utterly healthy, but a careful examination may reveal that they are infected.

Psittacosis can have a variety of symptoms, and therefore it is difficult to diagnose, especially in its early stages. Usually it starts with a heavy cold. Moisture drips from the nostrils, the bird gasps for air, and breathing is squeaky and hissing. The bird looks worn out and often has diarrhea. Before the disease

turns fatal, there are often symptoms of cramps and lameness.

Psittacosis can occur in a mild form, which can often be completely cured. However, be aware that recovered birds can be infectious for both bird and humans. Any case of the disease can pose a hazard, which is why you are legally required to report any suspicion of psittacosis to a veterinarian, the police, or the U.S. Public Health Service.

In humans, psittacosis starts with cold symptoms and can lead to a lung infection. In earlier times, the disease was dangerous. The advent of antibiotics has removed this danger, provided you get timely diagnosis and treatment. In the mid-1960s, many countries imposed strong restrictions on the import of hookbills. Imported parrots have to be quarantined for 30 days on arrival and are given a preventive treatment with chlortetracycline. Infected birds are treated 45 days with this drug.

Your Bird's Home Pharmacy

Heat source: infrared lamp (60–100 watt bulb).

Hospital cage: several commercial models are available. Ask your avian veterinarian or pet store manager for advice.

Environmental thermometer: buy one that's easy to read, so that you can accurately monitor the temperature in the hospital cage.

Cage covering: use a cage covering if you don't have a hospital cage. Towels or baby blankets are fine, as are a number of commercial covers. Drape these over an open bird cage.

Adhesive or masking tape: use one-half inch width.

Gauze bandage: use one-half inch roll.

Sterile gauze pads.

Cotton-tipped swabs.

Rubbing alcohol.

Needle-nosed pliers and/or tweezers.

Sharp scissors with rounded ends (baby nail scissors).

Feeding tubes: use 8F or 10F tubes, which many veterinarians carry. Ask your veterinarian to demonstrate the technique of tube feeding.

Syringes or plastic medicine droppers for administering oral medication.

Basic Medication and Other Necessities

Chlorox in a dilution of 6 ounces per gallon of water (excellent for cleaning concrete aviary floors; may be corrosive to bare metal).

Gevral Protein: Appetite loss (always mix with Mull Soy, which is also a good source of essential vitamins and minerals. Use one part Gevral Protein to three parts Mull Soy. Tube feed 2–3 ml, two to three times daily. Ask your veterinarian for details.

Kaopectate or Pepto-Bismol: Loose droppings and regurgitation. Soothes and coats the digestive tract. Helps to form a solid stool. Two to three drops every 4 hours, administered with a plastic medicine dropper.

Maalox or Digel: crop disorders. Soothes the inflammation and eliminates gas. Dosage: two to three drops every 4 hours.

Karo Syrup: dehydration and as provider of energy. Add four drops to 1 quart (1 liter) water. Administer 8–10 drops slowly in the mouth every 20–30 minutes with a plastic medicine dropper.

Monsel solution or styptic powder: bleed-ing (don't use styptic powder for areas near the beak).

Milk of magnesia: constipation. Dosage: three to five drops in the mouth with plastic dropper, twice daily for 2 days. Don't use milk of magnesia if your bird has kidney problems or a heart disease. Consult your veterinarian.

Mineral oil: constipation; crop impaction; egg binding. Use two drops in the mouth for 2 days with plastic dropper. Be very careful when administering the oil, as it can cause pneumonia and vitamin deficiency if it enters the breathing tubes and lungs.

Hydrogen peroxide, 3 percent, activated charcoal; milk of magnesia: poisoning. To induce vomiting, to absorb and to speed passage through the digestive tract. Ask your avian veterinarian for more details.

Goodwinol; mineral oil; Scalex; Eurax; Vaseline: scaly face and/or scaly leg.

Betadine; Domeboro solution; A&D ointment; Neosporin; Neopolycin; Mycitracin; Aquasol A: Skin irritations. Domeboro is used on a wet dressing: dissolve 1 teaspoon or tablet in a pint of water. A&D is excellent for small areas. Neosporin, Neopolycin, and Mycitracin contain antibiotics. Aquasol A is a cream and contains vitamin A. All these ointments and creams can be applied to the affected skin twice daily.

Lugol's iodine solution: thyroid enlargement (½ teaspoon of Lugol with 1 ounce of water; place one drop of this mixture in 1 ounce of drinking water for 2½ weeks).

Breeding Lovebirds

Most lovebird species are easy to breed, which accounts for much of their popularity with bird fanciers. They rank just behind cockatiels and budgerigars (parakeets) in this respect. Generally, you can count on successfully breeding and raising young if you provide your breeding stock with proper housing, feeding, and care. What's more, you'll find a ready market for the young, because the demand for lovebirds continues to exceed the supply. However, I urge that before you sell any fledglings (young that have left the nest), you first allow them to develop properly by housing them separately from the older birds and allowing them to fly in a good-sized run for at least 8–9 months.

Take careful note of the following advice before you attempt breeding: keep good breeding records. Even if you have a good memory, you can't rely on it to remember all the necessary details of each bird. An ordinary notebook will do. Set it up to record matings, eggs laid, hatchings, behavior, health, and other key data. Every time you check on the birds (regularly, but not too often!), record your findings in the notebook. I consider record keeping the foundation of any successful breeding program.

Good Breeding Stock

You need healthy parents to get healthy young. In other words, the parent birds must be selected with care.

Not to discourage you, but just because you acquired a male and female lovebird doesn't mean you can count on a successful breeding season. First of all, it's no foregone conclusion that birds will accept the partners we select for them. In general, birds bred in captivity won't present much of a problem in this respect. With imported, wild birds, however, it's best to let them select their own partners. For this purpose, place open bands of different colors on a number of males and females, and notice who pairs off with whom. If you see two birds that consistently keep each other's company, remove them from the group and put them in a separate cage or aviary. Nature will take care of the rest.

Birds must be of breeding age. They must be at least 10 months old (12 or 13 months is preferable). Birds older than 5–6 years of age should be retired from breeding.

Preparations

The best breeding results come about if you have several pairs of lovebirds, each of which has its own cage or aviary. If they remain within hearing distance, however, they'll stimulate each other's breeding efforts. I would attempt colony breeding only with the black-cheeked lovebirds and the Nyasa lovebirds. They make good aviary birds, together with other medium-sized birds of the parrot family. Do not skimp on space, and never put unpaired birds into the aviary. This leads to trouble. Secure mates quickly, or remove them from the aviary.

Birds need the right kind of feed to come into good breeding condition. If you were feeding only a seed mix during the winter, you can't expect them to be in top condition in spring. Seeds just don't meet their amino acid requirements, and if this need isn't met elsewhere, the results will be an unsuccessful breeding season.

Those of you using breeding cages (minimum size 3 feet 3½ inches × 3 feet 2 inches × 2 feet; 100 × 95 × 60 cm) should install them in a room that is light and airy and,

Breeding Lovebirds

above all, peaceful. Keep the indoor temperature at about 59°F (15°C). It can be somewhat higher, but not much lower. Humidity should be about 65 percent. This is very important and must be carefully kept in mind. When the humidity becomes too low, the risk of egg binding and hatching difficulties increases. (More often, however, egg binding is caused by a deficiency in the vitamin B complex.)

If you breed birds outdoors, there's not much you can do about the temperature. If you breed the tougher species (peach-faced, Fischer's, and Abyssinian), you can expect to begin as early as mid-April. The other species shouldn't get started until mid-May. Be aware, though, that the peach-faced lovebird seems to be ready to breed any time of the year; restrict this activity, to avoid egg binding, weak young, and other troubles.

Provide privacy in outdoor aviaries. Grow plants along the outside to create the peaceful atmosphere that's needed.

If you don't place the nestboxes in direct sunlight, you won't have to worry much about the humidity. If there is a long spell of dry or warm weather, gently spray the nestboxes with the garden hose each day.

Nesting Material

The mating urge of lovebirds can also be stimulated by furnishing good nestboxes (see page 29). Make the entrance of nestboxes big enough so that the birds don't lose their building materials when entering the nest. They seldom pick up lost building materials, which means much wasted effort. The entrance should have a diameter of about 2 inches (5 cm), or 3 inches (7 cm) for peach-faced lovebirds. The peach-faced seem to prefer boxes that have the entrance in the left or right upper corner, which gives them more privacy during breeding.

The basic material to furnish is fresh branches from fruit and willow trees, or from birch, mountain ash, linden, and poplar. You should provide fresh branches year-round (see page 34). Keep the branches from drying out by placing them in water. The birds will tear off bark strips to build their nest. Even when they seem to have completed the structure and have commenced laying eggs and breeding, they will still continue to build their nest. Lovebirds particularly like to have bundles of branches hung high near the roof of the aviary. If you throw branches on the ground, they will arouse very little interest.

For other materials, furnish grass, leaves, and bundles of spray millet. Present these in racks hung at a height of about 4 feet (120 cm). Most lovebirds carry building material in the "normal" way, in the beak, but the females of the Abyssinian lovebird, Madagascar lovebird, and red-faced lovebird often tuck nesting material anywhere between the

Masked and Fischer's lovebirds build two-compartment nests. The cross-section of this drawing shows that the upper compartment serves as entrance hall with nest opening. The lower compartment is the true nest where the young are hatched and raised.

Breeding Lovebirds

Nest building is clearly female's work. The illustration shows a masked lovebird holding several twigs in its beak.

body feathers, and peach-faced lovebirds carry large strips of bark and such tucked between the lower back and rump feathers.

Brooding

It can take weeks before birds actually commence building nests, so it's good not to lose hope too soon. Once birds are ready to breed, they can complete their nest in 4–5 days.

The first egg is laid within 10 days after mating, then one more every other day. The female usually starts brooding after the second egg has been laid.

After 5–6 days, you will be able to tell if the eggs are fertile. Hold each egg against the light, and you will clearly see a dark spot surrounded by some blood vessels. After a week, the eggshell becomes somewhat darker and has a bluish haze. Infertile eggs, by contrast, are transparent and turn yellow.

When eggs are infertile, it doesn't necessarily mean that the couple that produced them is infertile. Hereditary infertility exists but isn't very common. In most cases, you can attribute infertility to the physical condition of the parents. Make sure housing, feed, and care are up to par, and try again. If the second clutch of eggs is also infertile, try to get the female into the proper rhythm of the breeding process by transferring eggs from other nests with large clutches.

One type of "infertility" may be caused by human error; you may accidentally have put two females together! You will discover that this problem exists when you get a double clutch of infertile eggs.

The usual clutch contains four to six eggs. If you have larger clutches of properly fertilized eggs, place the extra eggs with other females that have fewer or infertile eggs. Keep track of the transferred eggs by marking them very softly with a black felt-tip pen.

You don't need to worry if transferring eggs requires giving them to a different species of lovebird. Most lovebirds make excellent foster parents and will raise the young of different species. The peach-faced lovebird, for example, will accept young from the masked lovebird and the Fischer's lovebird. If you don't have lovebird couples available for foster parenting, you can substitute cockatiels or even red-rumped parakeets (*Psephotus haematonotus*).

Be sure that the eggs you transfer are about the same age as those laid by the foster mother. The main reason for this is that the bird starts producing its "crop milk" during brooding so it can properly feed its young in the first days after hatching. If you place eggs that are ready to hatch under a female that has

Breeding Lovebirds

just started brooding, you will interfere with this natural process. As a result, the transferred young die or become so undernourished they never grow into healthy birds.

Depending on the species, brooding takes 22–25 days.

If chicks from large clutches are abandoned and you don't have foster parents available, you can try raising them by hand. I have seen people hand feed very young, naked birds with good results, but birds over 10 days old have a better chance to be raised successfully.

Hand-raised lovebirds usually become quite tame and devoted. Even as adults they will constantly seek human company.

Young hatchlings (up to 10 days old) should be fed day and night; start, say at 7 a.m. and continue every 2–3 hours. If you go to bed at midnight, you can do the night feedings at 3 and 5 a.m. (Uggh!) That's the closest you can come to the work of natural parents, who feed whenever the little crop is empty.

Young hatchlings will suck warm liquid food from a plastic spoon. Older birds can be fed with a hypodermic syringe with an 8F or 10F tube attached. Put the end of the tube into the crop very carefully before ejecting the food. (Ask your veterinarian or an experienced breeder to demonstrate this procedure.)

The best type of food to use, I have found, is Gerber's High Protein baby food, mixed with warm water 100°F (38°C); to a thin consistency; add some finely chopped sunflower seed (without hulls), a pinch of limestone, and a few drops of vitamin-mineral supplement. Keep the food warm; for birds under 10 days, keep the food at 89.6°F (32°C) or a little warmer.

Place hand-fed birds in a shoebox with the bottom covered with white felt or a similar absorbent soft material. Keep the young warm with a heat lamp, and prevent variation in temperature. As the birds feather out, you may gradually raise the temperature to 68°F (20°C). At this point, your birds will probably become quite restless and constantly try to leave the shoebox. It's best, then, to transfer them to a box cage.

Hand-raised birds are extremely tame and affectionate to the person who raised them.

Care of the Young

When young birds are 7–12 days old, it's time to think about banding them. The ring (band) size to use is 4.5 mm in diameter, which can be ordered through your bird club.

There are many advantages to banding, yet I hesitate to recommend it for your lovebirds. Installing the bands can cause injuries, although that can be prevented if you are coached by an experienced fancier. Wearing the bands can cause even bigger problems.

Lovebirds regard fresh corn as a delicacy. Here a wild Fischer's lovebird is enjoying a meal.

Breeding Lovebirds

Many parent birds peck at the rings of their offspring. The shiny rings are seen as foreign objects, and the parent birds will try to grasp and remove them at all costs. As a result, the legs of the young are wounded or even broken. Furthermore, constant pecking at rings by both parents and the young themselves cause jagged edges on the rings. These also can promote injuries, directly or when birds get hung up on branches and other objects. I have seen many a broken leg as a result.

A preventive measure to take is to blacken the bands with a felt-tip pen, so that they're less shiny. Also, rub some droppings on them, to give them a familiar scent. Ordinarily, this will make the rings less objectionable and the birds may leave them alone.

Nestlings will start to feather out at the end of the third week. At that point, watch out for females that peck feathers from the young. This may be all right if not overdone, and it generally stops when the young leave the nest. You can't wait long in serious cases, and you will have to transfer the young to foster parents. They will accept "adoptees" up to 3 weeks old. If you don't have foster parents available, discourage the pecking by rubbing the young birds with Bitter Apple or peppermint oil. For somewhat older birds, you can try removing the top of the nestbox (which is of course only practical if the birds are being raised in an aviary, as nestboxes on cages and such are usually hung on the outside, and birds could escape).

Young birds leave the nest at 6 weeks of age. By then the female has often started a second brood, but the male continues to feed the young until they are completely independent.

Well before the beginning of the breeding season, supply the special feed that parents like to offer their young, such as sprouted and soaked seed, spray millet, half-ripe grass seeds, small insects, commercial supplements, and egg feed. When birds leave the nest, the male will teach the young to eat regular feed, but supply the special feed until the young are completely independent, which takes about 2 weeks more.

Once the young are independent, provide a separate run or roomy cage if possible, and furnish the normal seed mix (see page 32), grit, water, and some of the special feed on which they were raised. They will go through their first molt at 3–4 months of age, a process that takes about 2 months. During that time, they are quite sensitive to cold and moisture, so the best place to keep them is in an indoor run.

Lovebirds in their habitat in Africa. Top: masked lovebirds having a drink at a puddle. Bottom: Nyasa lovebirds inspecting their future nest.

Understanding Lovebirds

An understanding of lovebird behavior is an integral part of their care and management. Besides, it is their interesting and exciting behavior that makes lovebirds so extremely popular, along with their natural colors and color mutations.

Lovebirds in the Wild

Many and detailed observations have been made of most lovebirds in the wild. The least-known lovebird is the black-collared, which is a forest bird and therefore difficult to observe and study. They live in small groups of up to 12 birds, high in the tops of trees, and they seldom come down to the forest floor. They feed principally on rice, half-ripe corn,

and figs. Experience has shown that these birds cannot be kept alive in captivity, so they are only of theoretical interest to the bird fancier. They were discovered in 1862 by Mr. O. J. Selby.

Other lovebirds live principally in open landscape and high in the mountains. They always stay quite close to water as they are heavy drinkers. In this, they differ from other types of parrots and parakeets, which drink water only rarely. Lovebirds are adapted to living close to humans and are seen in great numbers on cultivated fields, to the understandable annoyance of the local farmers.

The peach-faced lovebird has a rather large range on the west coast of Southwestern Af-

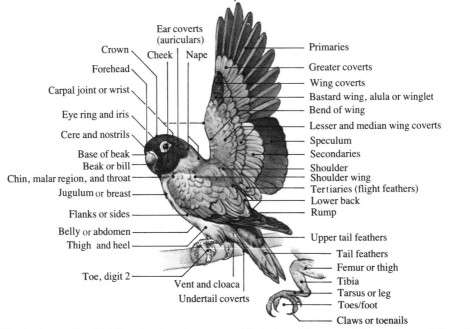

Crown
Ear coverts (auriculars)
Cheek | Nape
Forehead
Carpal joint or wrist
Eye ring and iris
Cere and nostrils
Base of beak
Beak or bill
Chin, malar region, and throat
Jugulum or breast
Flanks or sides
Belly or abdomen
Thigh and heel
Toe, digit 2
Vent and cloaca
Undertail coverts

Primaries
Greater coverts
Wing coverts
Bastard wing, alula or winglet
Bend of wing
Lesser and median wing coverts
Speculum
Secondaries
Shoulder
Shoulder wing
Tertiaries (flight feathers)
Lower back
Rump
Upper tail feathers
Tail feathers
Femur or thigh
Tibia
Tarsus or leg
Toes/foot
Claws or toenails

What is where on a lovebird? Knowing the different parts of the body and the areas of plumage is especially useful when talking with your avian veterinarian.

Understanding Lovebirds

rica, where small flocks can be found high in the mountains up to 5000 feet (1500 m) above sea level. The masked lovebird, by contrast, has a restricted range, as does the Fischer's. Their combined range is barely 100 miles (160 km). Both species live in small groups, not only in meadowland, but also high in the mountains, up to an altitude of 5500 feet (1650 m). The Nyasa lovebird will range even higher; they have been sighted at an altitude of 6300 feet (1900 m).

The Abyssinian moves in small flocks of 4–20 birds through the plateaus and the light forests and can be found up to an altitude of an amazing 10,000 feet (3000 m). It likes to snack on the berries of juniper bushes and feast on the fruit of fig trees, which they consider a delicacy. This species seems to be least attracted to humans. It is considerably less likely to spread into human habitations than, for example, the red-faced and the Madagascar.

Madagascar lovebirds are common especially along the shore of Madagascar. Some years ago it was introduced on Mauritius, the Comoro Islands, Rodriguez, Zanzibar, Mafia Island, and the Seychelles.

The red-faced lovebird has the biggest range of all—the entire savanna region of Central Africa. It lives in small groups that feed on figs, berries, grass and weed seed, and occasionally grain. During most of the day, they feed on the ground and are great walkers that constantly chatter.

Nests in the Wild

Wild birds don't appear to be choosy when picking a nesting place. I have discovered the strangest sites: under the eaves of huts, under the watering troughs of cattle, and even on the roof of an abandoned chicken coop. Peach-faced lovebirds have been found under gutters, on window sills, and in other niches of inhabited houses and other buildings. Lovebirds will also use abandoned bird nests, especially those of weaver birds. Most birds nonetheless prefer proper hollows in the baobab and other trees.

The most accomplished architects of all the lovebird species are the Fischer's and the masked. I think their accomplishments are exceeded only by the gigantic nest-building activity of the Quaker or monk parakeet (*Myiopsitta monachus*) from South America (which has been introduced to Puerto Rico and the northeastern United States).

The two lovebird species can modify large openings and even large enclosures, which they fill with building material and adapt to their needs. Their nests always have two "rooms": a hall with entrance hole and a true breeding room, in which they lay their eggs and raise their young.

The speed at which lovebirds build their nests varies with the availability of suitable building material. They can finish in 10–14 days, but I know of cases when they took a month or more.

Flight

Lovebirds, with their short, rounded wings, are strong, fast, and extremely maneuverable fliers. In the wild, they spend several miles on the wing each day, which is good to remember when we raise them in cages and aviaries!

In captivity, they adapt to limited flight possibilities by stretching on a perch and beating their wings with a strong and rapid motion. (Actually, this behavior is rather

Understanding Lovebirds

Very few cages and aviaries have enough room for birds to fly to their heart's content. Caged birds satisfy their urge to fly by sitting on a perch and beating their wings with strong, fast movements.

common with all cage and aviary birds in captivity.) During the breeding season, you can often see a lovebird female leave the nest, especially when she is brooding, just to "stretch her wings" with these flight simulations.

Social Behavior

Lovebirds in the wild tend to move in small groups, but this can change drastically after the breeding season, particularly if it has been fruitful. Then you can see flocks of more than a hundred birds. Even in such large flocks, the individual couples maintain a strong bond. They form this pair bond early, after the first molt, and maintain it for life.

In the wild as well as in captivity, the partners will constantly groom one another, especially in spots where a bird can't reach to groom itself. It is touching to see two birds side by side on a branch lovingly going through each other's feathers. The head and neck especially are gone over with delicate movements of the beak. The young are also

groomed by their parents, who remove bits of dirt and loose feathers with their bills.

Paired lovebirds feed one another from the crop, not only before and during the breeding season, but throughout the year. The food is moved from the crop by pumplike movements, and the half-digested material is fed to the partner. Generally, the male takes in more food this way than the female. During the breeding season this behavior becomes more intense, and it seems to stimulate sexual behavior.

Later, the behavior takes on a more practical cast, when the male feeds his mate on the nest while she is brooding eggs or tending to newly hatched young. She, in turn, feeds the nestlings.

Sometimes a male becomes impatient at mating time and discontinues grooming and feeding the hen and attempts to copulate. It can then happen that the female will reject her mate, approaching from the side, with a few solid whacks with the beak. She opens the beak as she does this and makes a sound that is much like hissing. The male shields himself

Mutual preening of the feathers concentrates on areas that a bird cannot reach with its own beak.

Understanding Lovebirds

Mutual preening and feeding intensify during the breeding season.

with one of his wings and makes some beating movements or withdraws.

You won't see this mating behavior if you don't have a true male and female couple. At first, two males may sit side by side and exhibit much of the same behavior as true couples. The only indication that it isn't a true couple is that they make no attempt to build a nest, which is the specialty of the female.

There are fewer clues in the case of a couple formed by two females. They can lead you by the nose for a long time, because they groom, feed, and approach one another slowly, then mount and mimic copulation. They will even build a nest. Until egg-laying time, one of the birds takes on a clearly masculine role, and the other the feminine. After completion of the nest, the eggs are laid, and the double clutch gives the deception away.

Aggression

Don't let the name "lovebird" mislead you, because even among lovebirds there isn't always peace and harmony. They can attack one another viciously, especially when newcomers are introduced into a cage or aviary. If a newcomer interferes with the con-

struction of a nest or the brooding of some eggs, heavy blows can fall from a wing or bites from a beak until the intruder retreats. There are cases of pugnacious intruders that won't stop fighting, and events can degenerate into a real battle in which both birds start shoving and hissing. If that doesn't impress, they commence a real beak fight, and believe me, this can be anything but gentle. It is fierce and unbridled. Small wounds may result, which naturally should be treated immediately. This is why it is inadvisable to place an extra male or female in a group aviary.

Vocalization

It's well known that lovebirds can make sounds that don't exactly please the ears. One sharp sounding call is the so-called contact call. As the name indicates, the purpose of this call is to keep partners and young in touch, even when they move in groups to drinking and eating areas. It also keeps the flock together. If foreign birds should enter a flock, members of the group recognize the outsiders immediately. If there is enough feed and if the young have not yet formed definitive pairs and other conditions are favorable, new birds aren't automatically rejected and may be considered as mates. If all pairs have been formed, however, chances are that outsiders will be rejected because they could disturb the peace of the group.

Further, lovebirds have a so-called alarm call, which even humans can recognize as such. They use this call when danger is suspected or evident (birds of prey or a dominant member of the group).

Even more piercing is the "fear call" with which you are commonly confronted if you take a bird that doesn't know you well into your hand. Lovebirds clearly find this stressful (see page 17). They have this fear call even as nestlings, and you will hear it, for example, if you put a bird that fell from the nest back where it came from.

Nevertheless, you can note a peaceable, soft, relaxed twitter, especially in a quiet noontime period, when the birds actually seem to sing to themselves.

Body Movements

Lovebirds make some typical body movements that communicate useful information to the observant pet owner. Many of these movements are most marked in the peach-faced lovebird.

Head Movements from Left to Right with Short, Small Strokes

This behavior occurs most often when the bird is upset about something, as when a fly or mosquito is circling its head and won't go away or when something sticks to a bird's beak and can't be removed with its claws.

A somewhat different head movement is the swaying that occurs during the mating dance. However, when a bird becomes annoyed during mating, it can exhibit this same short, small head movement.

Cleaning the Beak

This behavior occurs mainly after a bird has eaten fruit or some other sticky food or when it has eaten seed mixed with husks that cleave to the beak. You can observe this cleaning, which is performed by rubbing the beak with a leg or against a branch. The same behavior can also be a displacement activity, a type of nervous reaction. Males ready to

mate can become quite nervous and may engage in this activity repeatedly, especially if it appears that the female is not yet ready to mate. Sometimes the behavior occurs without an apparent reason.

Bowing and Stretching

Birds will stretch to their greatest possible height to make an impression on another bird, for a number of reasons, most generally aggressive in nature. If the other party is impressed, it will shyly make a bow or nervous nods as a sign of submission. During a mating dance, both birds take turns showing this behavior.

Swaying the Head

This behavior is carried out in a quiet, steady, slow rhythm, principally during the mating dance. The head is moved slowly from right to left so that first one cheek and then the other is turned toward the partner.

Wing Beating

This behavior can be part of the mating dance, but is also exhibited at other times (see page 67). It is interesting that this wing beating is especially exhibited by lovebird species in which the males have black feathers on the lower wing. The behavior can also serve as a warning to scare away a true enemy or just another lovebird that has approached too closely.

Raised Feathers with Shaking Motions

This is more behavior of the mating season that serves to impress. It is also used to warn away rival birds. The wings are often held away from the body for 4–5 seconds. In seri-

Understanding Lovebirds

ous conflicts, the wings may be completely outstretched or folded over the back.

Extreme Drooping of the Wings

This behavior displays a seemingly unnatural position and is generally a sign that the bird doesn't feel well. It can also be a gesture to generate sympathy. Males sometimes exhibit this behavior if they are dominated by their partners.

Wing Whirring

Here the bird appears to fly while remaining perched on a branch (see page 68). It is a sign that the bird feels great or wants to inform others that it is important. It can also be a sign of agitation, and then the mantle feathers are spread.

Charging

When birds make charging movements with the beak, this can be regarded as an offensive or defensive maneuver. When charging, the head and back are held low, the tail is spread, and the head feathers are fluffed. When the birds almost touch one another (there is no actual bodily contact), the feathers smooth out.

Beak Fencing

This behavior is usually a sign that a bird wants to bite and is often accompanied by a screech. It leads to an actual attack directed at the legs or toes of another bird. The victim also makes fencing motions and directs these at the opponent's beak. Beak fencing occurs more often if too many birds are crowded together in a small enclosure, like a shipping crate. If this happens in overcrowded aviaries and cages, it can recur repeatedly and interfere markedly with the peace and harmony of the bird population.

Raised Tail

This is a sign of self-confidence.

Lowered Tail

This usually indicates a sick bird. This behavior can also occur during mating, when it signals surrender. Only males exhibit the behavior as females consistently dominate the males.

Lovebird Species

Lovebirds got their name because of their affectionate natures, although the females of the black-winged or Abyssinian lovebird (*Agapornis taranta taranta*) and the Madagascar or gray-headed lovebird (*Agapornis cana cana*) are the dominant sex, as they select the nest side and defend this against other birds. They even snap at their mates. Mutual preening of these two species is rather one-sided.

Lovebirds are delightful animals, whether kept in a roomy cage, a large aviary or observed in the wild. Generally speaking, they breed quite readily and capture your heart with their adorable chatter. In the wild they often nest in loose colonies, and one tree may shelter many nests.

They are found in the tropical parts of Africa and on the island of Madagascar. *Agapornis* species are recognized by their short, rounded tails. On the average, the birds are about 5–6 inches (12.5–15 cm) long. Although most of their plumage is green, we have recognized species that have some yellow, red, and blue feathers. Lovebirds live in small groups in forests, plains, and swamps; some species live in mountainous regions up to approximately 10,000 feet (3000 m) above sea level; others frequent the open fields, but all species in this genus can be found south of 13 degrees north latitude.

Agapornis species feed on various types of grass seeds, sweet berries, fruit, and a variety of grains and grass; in captivity they should be offered a number of different seeds (page 32), as well as groats, dry and water-soaked rice, berries, and new green twigs (page 33). In addition, the birds should be offered cuttlefish bone, gravel, and oyster grit daily (page 36).

Agapornis species use fresh nesting material; in fact, they use quite a lot to construct their nests. Several species even transport these building materials between their back and/or chest feathers (page 60). Lovebirds live and breed in colonies, although during the breeding period some will break away into small groups to share the "good and bad" together. Even in these smaller groups some disharmony might occur but to a lesser degree than in the larger colony. In each colony one of the stronger males will act as leader to intervene successfully if and when little disagreements present themselves. This will take place even in an aviary housing several couples of a particular kind. I have observed that these minor arguments are mostly restricted to evening quarrels, for rarely will these birds steal nesting material or food from each other; in any event, their breeding habits are rarely affected by these little upsets.

The White Eye-Ring Group

Masked Lovebird
Agapornis personata personata Reichenow, 1887
Color photographs: pages 9, 28, and 64, and back cover

Lovebird Species

Description: Head is blackish brown with yellow collar. Throat and chest are yellow with an orange-red glow. The balance of the body is primarily green, with the exception of the rump, which is bluish, and the tail, which shows a black and red band shortly before the ends on the outer feathers. The brown eyes are encircled with a wide white periophthalmic ring; the legs are gray. The bill is red.

The young look like their parents, although their coloring is somewhat duller and the black in the plumage is not very bright.

Length: 6–6¼ inches (15–15.7 cm).

Distribution: Northeast Tanzania, southeast of Lake Manyara.

Habitat: Nomadic; it survives on the seeds of available trees and roosts in the crevices and crannies of baobabs. This bird will nest in swifts' nests and breeds in the approximately 3-inch (7½-cm) space between the tiles of a roof and the boards underneath. Often they will also nest under iron roofs, which retain much of the heat radiated by the sun. They brood in colonies. The construction of the nest itself is an action exclusive to the hen. I have kept three pairs together in one aviary, provided them with 10 nesting boxes to avoid quarreling, and was rewarded with success. If it is a warm and sunny spring, hose off the nestboxes each morning and (early) evening, but take care that none of the water actually seeps inside.

Captivity: Males often scratch their heads with their feet prior to mating; females line the nests; they also weigh more than males—2 versus 1.8 ounces (56 versus 50 grams). The hen lays three to four eggs; incubation time is 21–23 days. The young leave the nest at 44–45 days of age. Provide more boxes than there are bird pairs. The hen enjoys a good supply of willow twigs.

There are quite a few color mutations, the blue mutation being the best known. The collar, chest, and belly of this recessive mutation are an off-white; the head is black. The beak is horn colored.

Fischer's Lovebird

Agapornis personata fischeri Reichenow, 1887

Color photographs: inside front cover, pages 9 and 63, and inside back cover

Description: The back, chest, and wings are green; the neck is a golden yellow, and the cheeks and throat are orange. The top of the head is olive green, the forehead a lovely tomato red. The feathers just above the tail are blue; the tail is green with sky-blue tips with an indistinct black band shortly before the end. The roots of the outermost feathers of the wings are brownish red underneath. Eyes are brown, beak red, and legs slate blue.

The offspring look much like the parents except that their colors are somewhat duller and the base of the upper mandible has brown markings.

Length: 4 inches (10 cm).

Distribution: South and southeast of Lake Victoria; East Africa north of Tanzania.

Habitat: This species lives at elevations of 3200–4900 feet (1000–1500 m) in small flocks. Their flight is straight and fast; in flight, the rustling sound of their wings can be heard, as can their high-pitched chirping. The species prefers to live in isolated clumps of trees with grass plains between them.

Captivity: This species is very sociable in an aviary. The hen lays four to six eggs; it takes 3–3½ weeks for the eggs to hatch. After 35–37 days the young will fly from the nest. After another 10

days, the youngsters are totally independent, and it is then best to separate them from the parents.

An important color mutation is the blue variety. This mutation is somewhat smaller than the wild bird and has an extremely pale gray head. It was first bred by R. Horsham in South Africa around 1957. In 1959, it was bred in San Francisco, California, by Dr. F. B. Warford.

Black-cheeked Lovebird

Agapornis personata nigrigenis W. L. Sclater, 1906

Color photographs: pages 9 and 45

Description: The overall color is green; forehead and cheeks are dark brown to black; throat sides and rear of the head are yellow-greenish; throat is orange with a brown glow; there is a vague pink blotch on the chest. The eye ring is white. Eyes are brown, beak red, and legs gray. The female is a little duller.

The young look very much like the parents, although in their early life their colors are considerably duller. Some fledglings have black spots on the bills.

Length: 4½ inches (11 cm).

Distribution: A small region in the northern portion of Zimbabwe, around the Zambezi River and the Victoria waterfalls (Africa).

Habitat: In the wild they live in all forests except evergreen; they are cheerful and fast and not par-

ticularly timid. I have observed these birds taking baths early in the morning and late in the afternoon in little streams and small waterfalls. Their distribution is relatively limited, being around 80 miles (130 km) in diameter.

Captivity: These lovebirds have become rare in aviculture due to export restrictions in their country of origin. They are excellent breeders. They are sweet and peaceful, even when housed with fellow species or other exotic birds. The hen lays four to six, sometimes two to eight eggs. Both sexes incubate the eggs; incubation time is 16–21 days. After about 30 days the young fly out. The male does not feed the hen while she is sitting on the eggs. No color mutations are known.

Nyasa Lovebird

Agapornis personata lilianae Shelley, 1894

Color photographs: front cover, and pages 9, 45, and 64

Description: The bird is primarily green in color, the underside being a little lighter; the forehead and the crown are tomato red, and the cheeks and throat are paler, more of an orange-red color. The green tail has a yellowish tint at the base and a dark band shortly before the tip. The tail is green at the tip, but ends in a base that turns to an orange-red. The beak is red, the feet and legs are grayish brown, and the eyes are brown. The female is identical to the male, although sometimes the red on her head is a little less bright. Her eyes may be a shade lighter. There is also a slight weight difference between the sexes, the female weighing about 1½ ounces (43 grams) and the male about 1¼ ounce (35 grams). The offspring is duller in color, with the green and red colors somewhat darker. The color of the cheeks is still a little vague.

Length: 4¼ inches (11 cm).

Distribution: Southern Tanzania, northern Zimbabwe, eastern Malawi, and northwestern Mozambique.

Habitat: There is very little to say about their life in the wild; it is best to refer to the other subspecies that have a white eye ring. They do prefer to live in close proximity to water, such as near large rivers. Nevertheless, they may be found in various elevations ranging from 1600 to 4900 feet (500–1500 m) above sea level. Their habitat practically borders that of the *A. p. nigrigenis* yet the two species do not cross-breed with each other, even though there may be only a strip of 50 miles (80 k) between their homes. Outside the breeding period, the Nyasa lovebirds wander about in groups of 30–40 birds. One can hear their shrill cries as they fly overhead searching for water and food. The birds bring nesting materials to the nest by means of their beak. Once the nest has been completed, and quite often this includes a sort of overhang, the female will lay between three and five white eggs, which she will hatch in about 3 weeks. The male will feed her and also helps in rearing the chicks once they have flown out of the nest at about 30–35 days.

Captivity: This species is very sociable in an aviary and friendly toward birds of similar size. The hen lays four to six white eggs which take 3 to 3½ weeks to hatch. After 35 to 37 days the young will fly from the nest. After another 10 days, the youngsters are totally independent and it is then best to separate them from the parents. Provide more nest boxes than there are bird pairs. Nyasa lovebirds are excellent breeders and can rear three clutches per season.

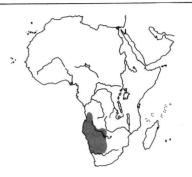

The Intermediate Groups

Peach-faced Lovebird

Agapornis roseicollis roseicollis (Vieillot), 1817

Color photographs: pages 10, 27, and 46

Description: The male has a soft pinkish red forehead, cheeks, chin, and throat, as well as an area just above the chest (the forehead being the darkest). Most of the rest of the bird is bright green, including the underside, which is somewhat lighter with a hint of yellow. Rump and covering feathers above the tail are bright light blue; on the green tail there are some black and rust-colored feathers. The eyes are brown, the beak is yellow to very light green, and the feet and legs are greenish gray. There is a faint ring around the eyes.

The female is difficult to distinguish. The green and blue colors and particularly the orange in the tail are considerably less sharp than the male's colors; the beak is darker in color. Immature birds are grayish green and lack the red coloring on the forehead.

Length: 6–7 inches (16–18 cm). It is the largest of the lovebirds. Full-grown hens are larger than males.

Distribution: Southwestern Africa. There are two subspecies: *A. r. roseicollis*, which was probably discovered and documented by about 1817; *A. r. catumbella*, discovered in 1955 and recognized by its colors.

Lovebird Species

Habitat: Comparatively small groups, mostly in areas that are dry and grow leaf-shedding trees; usually near a body of water.

Captivity: This species is supposedly the first to have been seen transporting nest-building materials between its back and rump feathers. The female lays four to five eggs. After 30–38 days the young fly out of the nest but will continue to be fed (mostly by the father) for some time, while the mother starts laying new eggs or looks for a new nesting box. They are excellent breeders and can breed and rear three clutches per season. Independent young should be housed in a separate, roomy aviary. Besides par blue mutations, which can also be found in the wild (and are recessive), there are many other mutations.

The Sexually Dimorphic Group

Abyssinian Lovebird or Black-winged Lovebird

Agapornis taranta taranta (Stanley), 1814

Color photograph: page 10

Description: Both sexes are grass green; the male has a red brow. The periophthalmic ring is also red in the male, greenish in the female. The tail is black tipped. The feathers just below the tail show a yellow glow, as does the curve of the wings.

Rump and feathers immediately above the tail are light green, as is the entire top of the bird; the underside is light green also. In the male the feathers under the wings are black; in females, greenish or sometimes brownish black. Immature birds look like their mother, except for the beak, which will remain brownish yellow until a few weeks later, when it will turn red. The iris of the adult bird is brown.

Length: 6–6.5 inches (15–16.5 cm).

Distribution: Southern Eritrea and southwestern highlands of Ethiopia. There are two subspecies: *A. t. taranta*, which is a little larger than *A. t. nana*. The latter subspecies has shorter wings and a small bill.

Habitat: The birds in this species generally live together in small groups. The nest is used as a year-round roost, making the population rather stationary. Their singing is not at all offensive, apart from the little screeching notes they tend to include occasionally. If they are upset they may even give voice to it at night! Their song is soft but should not be compared to that of songbirds. They prefer the sparse woods of the highlands and sometimes can be found at a height of 6000–10,000 feet (1800–3000 m) above sea level. Consequently, they are accustomed to cold weather and can be kept in the outside aviary even during the winter, provided there is a draft-free and dry night shelter available. It is desirable to hang a few sleeping boxes in the shelter as lovebirds prefer to spend the night in these.

Captivity: The female lays between three and six eggs; they are laid every other day. Depending upon the weather it will take 24–26 days for the eggs to hatch. This species seldom builds a nest; I provide a thick layer of moist wood shavings, which I press down firmly. The nesting box measures 10 inches long × 6 inches deep × 7 inches high (25½ × 15½ × 18 cm); these are inside measurements. It is advisable to separate the young from their parents once they have become adults to avoid accidents.

Lovebird Species

Madagascar Lovebird or Gray-headed Lovebird

Agapornis cana cana (Gmelin), 1788

Color photograph: page 10

Description: The upper part is green. The head, cheeks, throat, neck, and parts of the shoulder and chest are whitish gray. Underparts are light grass green; the wings are dark green. The tail is green with black feather tips. The chest has a hazy yellow glow that becomes darker toward the wings and underside. The beak is whitish gray, the eyes brown, and the legs pale gray. The female is green with green underwing coverts. Young males are a more intense green on the back and wings, and the gray can be seen quite early in life, sometimes while they are still in the nest.

Length: 5½ inches (14 cm).

Distribution: Malagasy Republic (formerly Madagascar); introduced to Rodriguez Island, Mauritius, Comoro Islands, Seychelles, Zanzibar, and Mafia Island. There are two subspecies: *A. c. cana* and *A. c. ablectanea*—a subspecies found only in the southwest region of Malagasy. The "trademark" of this bird is the brighter gray colors of its head, neck, and chest and the sharper greens of its wings and underside.

Habitat: This species often travels in large flocks of 150 or more birds, often causing considerable damage to farmland. They live mostly along the edge of forests, where there are trees that shed their leaves. The birds use shallow holes in trees as well as crevices in rocks and other places to build their nests, with tree holes the most popular and common. The female lays from four to six white eggs. In the wild I have seen nests that contained as many as 11 eggs.

Captivity: This species is primarily a seasonal breeder: November and December. As the birds catch cold easily, they are best kept in indoor aviaries. The female will use a budgerigar nestbox and will make a little "cushion" of various materials (dried leaves chewed into the desired shape and size) in the hollow of the nest. Grass, straw, strips of newspaper, bark of willow and fruit trees, larch needles, and other materials are also accepted. Incubation time is 22 days. The young leave the nest when about 5 weeks old. There have been no color mutations reported with this species. Only when these lovebirds are kept in a roomy aviary will they breed, although even then there are no guarantees. Acclimatization of the birds is most important, for these birds can still present problems before they have adjusted to their new lodging and become comfortable with their environment.

Red-faced Lovebird

Agapornis pullaria pullaria Linnaeus, 1758

Color photograph: page 10.

Description: The male is predominantly green, darker on top than underneath, where often a yellowish glow can be seen. The forehead, cheeks, and throat are tomato red, and the beak is scarlet. The narrow ring around the eyes is white, yellow, or bluish in color. The rump is sky blue, but the covering feathers just above the tail are green. The primary flight feathers have black tips; the curve (bend) of the wings is black with blue. The center tail feathers are green; the rest of the tail feathers are red with a black band a little before the tips, but the tips themselves are green. Feet and legs are greenish gray, and the covering feathers under the wings are black. The female's face is orange rather than tomato red, and this colored area is usually smaller than the male's. The covering feathers under the wings are green. The immature birds resemble the hen, although the covering feathers under the wings quickly become black in the young males. The bill is orange-red with a yellow tip.

Length: 6 inches (15 cm).

Distribution: Sierra Leone, Cameroons, northern Angola, Uganda, and Rwanda (Africa). Although not all ornithologists agree, most divide this species into two subspecies, namely, *A. p. pullaria*, a native of Western equatorial Africa and countries east of Sierra Leone to Lake Albert (Uganda), northern Angola, and south to Rwanda; *A. p. ungandae*, from Uganda and Rwanda.

Habitat: Wooded regions in large flocks. They feed on grass seeds, leaf buds, figs, millets, or corn, generally leaving fields in a ravaged state. They carve their nests in the large, still inhabited tree nests of termites or in termite hills, a job primarily performed by the female. The "lodgings" should be imagined as a small tunnel with a widened, fairly round cavity, called a kettle.

Captivity: Very hard to breed. The best method is using a big drum filled with moistened moss and then left to dry. Branches and twigs should be arranged on top and around it. The female lays four to seven eggs; incubation time is 24 days. The young leave the nest when 6–7 weeks old.

Swindern's Black-collared Lovebird

Agapornis swinderniana swinderniana (Kuhl), 1820

Description: Head is grass green with somewhat less bright cheeks. The underside is light green with a yellowish glow at the throat. The back is mostly green; the rump and area just above the tail are a deep blue. The tail is green with some red at the base and black at the tips. There is a black curved band that runs along the back of the neck, with a yellowish narrower band behind it that forms a vague circle around the entire neck. Their brown eyes contain a bright yellow iris. Their beaks are grayish; their feet are dark gray. The young birds do not have the black collar, and the yellowish band around the neck is extremely vague. Very little is known about the offspring before they leave the nest.

Length: 5 inches (13 cm).

Distribution: Liberia. Many ornithologists recognize three subspecies: *A. s. swinderniana*, from Liberia; *A. s. zenkeri*, from Cameroon to Central Zaire (formerly the Congo); and *A. s. emini*, from the Ituri and Semliki districts of Zaire.

Habitat: This is the only species that does not live at the edge, but rather in the thick of the forest, preferably the dense jungle. The species prefers figs above all else, although corn, grass seeds, small fruits, and the remains of insects have been found in the stomachs of dead specimens.

Very little is known about their breeding habits. It is supposed that they use convenient little nooks and that their eggs are pure white.

Captivity: There has been a report of a Belgian missionary, Father Hutsbout, who had a successful experience with these birds in captivity. He declared that he was unable to keep the birds alive unless he fed them a diet of wild figs. He attempted to mix these fruits with spray millet in order to get them to eat the seed, but to no avail. They would peck at palm nuts and peanuts, but if the figs were not provided for them to eat, they died within 3 or 4 days. Apart from this one reported incident, there have been no other accounts of success with these lovebirds in captivity. The risk involved in keeping this variety seems hardly worth taking, as it will probably result in the demise of many birds before success is achieved.

Index

79

Index

Sources of Information

Books

Alderton, David: *Lovebirds*, South Group, Ltd., Leicester, England, 1981.

Brockmann, J., and Latermann, W.: *Agaporniden*, Verlag Eugen Ulmer, Stuttgart, 1981.

Deimer, Petra: *Parrots*, Barron's, Woodbury, New York, 1983.

Forshaw, Joseph M.: *Parrots of the World*, David & Charles, Newton Abbot, London, 1978.

Gerstenfeld, Sheldon: *The Bird Care Book*, Addison Wesley, Reading, Massachusetts, 1981.

Hayward, Jim: *Lovebirds and Their Colour Mutations*, Blandford Press, Poole, Dorset, England, 1979.

Low, Rosemary: *Parrots, Their Care and Breeding*, Blandford Press, Poole, Dorset, England, 1980.

Smith, George A.: *Lovebirds and Related Parrots*, Paul Elek Ltd., London, 1979.

Vriends, Matthew M.: *Simon & Schuster's Guide to Pet Birds*, Simon & Schuster, New York, 1984.

Magazines (also see Societies)

American Cage Bird Magazine, Inc.
One Glamore Court
Smithtown, NY 11787

Bird Talk
P.O. Box 3940
San Clemente, CA 92672

Societies

African Lovebird Society
P.O. Box 142
San Marcos, CA 92069
(publishes a monthly journal)

American Federation of Aviculture
2208 "A" Artesia Boulevard
Redondo Beach, CA 90278
(publishes the bimonthly "The A.F.A. Watchbird," undoubtedly the best avicultural magazine around)

National Parrot Association
8 North Hoffman Lane
Hauppauge, NY 11788
(publishes a bimonthly journal)

The Avicultural Society of America, Inc.
P.O. Box 157
Stanton, CA 90680
(publishes a monthly bulletin)